ORCHESTRAL PERCUSSION
TECHNIQUE

500.

Orchestral Percussion Technique

BY

JAMES BLADES

Second Edition

London

OXFORD UNIVERSITY PRESS

OXFORD   NEW YORK

Oxford University Press, Walton Street, Oxford 0X2 6DP

Oxford London Glasgow New York
Toronto Melbourne Wellington Cape Town
Ibadan Nairobi Dar Es Salaam Lusaka
Kuala Lumpur Singapore Jakarta Hong Kong Tokyo
Delhi Bombay Calcutta Madras Karachi

ISBN 0 19 318803 1

First published 1961
Second edition 1973
Revised impression 1977

Printed in Great Britain

CONTENTS

PERCUSSION INSTRUMENTS OF DEFINITE PITCH
(THE TUNED PERCUSSION)

PREFACE

The subject of this book has fascinated me since boyhood, and I have cherished the instruments of percussion since I became the possessor of a toy drum. They in turn have supported me, both morally and physically, throughout an interesting career.

To all who are interested in the technique of percussion I tender my good wishes, and I offer them in the pages that follow such professional information and advice as my ability will allow.

My thanks are given to the many colleagues who have helped me with their remarks and advice, and also to the composers — too numerous to mention — whose works have been an inspiration to me.

The help of my wife in correcting and typing has been invaluable.

James Blades

Note to the Second Edition

I have been very pleased at the general response to this little book. During the years which have passed since it was first published, there have been many changes in the field of orchestral percussion, and I have made a number of amendments which seemed necessary to take account of these.

INTRODUCTION

Percussion — *percutio* — 'the act of striking'. To acquire the art of striking is the most important factor in percussion technique. To some, it may seem simpler to produce a sound from a percussion instrument than to set in motion the vibrations of a stringed or wind instrument. But in fact to produce the correct sound by striking can only be accomplished by diligent practice, and by appreciation of the special musical qualities and possibilities of all the orchestral percussion instruments, which range from the humble triangle to the regal kettledrum.

Orchestral percussion instruments are normally divided into three groups:

The percussion instruments of indefinite pitch, including the side drum, tenor drum, bass drum, cymbals, tam-tam, triangle, tambourine, castanets, wood blocks, jingles, anvil, whip, etc.

The timpani. Descendants of the cavalry kettledrums, they have been used in orchestral compositions for some three hundred years. A pair was customary in the early Classical period, increasing to two pairs and sets of three with the Romantic composers, whilst today it is not uncommon to see in full use a set of four or more pedal timpani.

The tuned percussion, principally the glockenspiel, xylophone, marimba, vibraphone, and tubular bells. All of the instruments in the three groups are to be found in the full orchestra, and all occur from time to time in small orchestras also. (I have not discussed the celeste, which is a keyboard instrument, or the cimbalom — an elaborate dulcimer.)

PERCUSSION INSTRUMENTS
OF INDEFINITE PITCH

THE SIDE (SNARE) DRUM

FR. *CAISSE CLAIRE*; GER. *KLEINE TROMMEL*;
IT. *TAMBURO*

A sound technique on the side drum assists a good performance on other percussion instruments. In company with the majority of percussion instruments, the side drum requires a great deal of basic practice. To all within earshot, the attendant 'tap-tap' can become — to say the least — a trifle disturbing; so the use of a practice pad is advised. There are several excellent pads on the market; all rest firmly on the table, some also fit neatly on to the side drum or stand. If funds are limited, a practice pad can be easily made for little outlay.

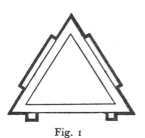

Fig. 1

Join three pieces of ¾ in. wood, each 8 in. square.

Fix a circular cork mat to side one and (for discreet playing) a circular rubber disc to side two. For insulation add rubber buffers to the base. This angled pad is suitable for the traditional grip of the drumsticks *(qv.)*. If the matched grip is used, only sides one and two are necessary and these may be joined back to back. If a side drum is 'muted' for practice purposes by releasing the snares and placing a soft household duster on the playing head the tone is similar to that of a practice pad. (The absence of snares dispels any impression of premature virtuosity.)

An ideal side drum is one measuring 14 in. in diameter and 5 in. in depth. The modern trend, even in the large orchestra, is for a clearly defined crisp sound. A drum deeper than 5 in. can sound 'tubby', and one larger than 14 in. in diameter may prove over-resonant. Well-matched and evenly-tensioned heads are essential: the 'batter' head to be slightly stouter than the lower (snare) head. For normal purposes the lower head is usually a shade tighter than the upper head. This, and the choice of wood or metal shell, is a matter of personal taste, as is the choice of snares and the use of calf or plastic heads. The advantage of the plastic head is its durability, and that it is not affected by changing atmospheric conditions. On the other hand certain players claim a greater range of dynamics and a silkier tone from a calf head, and use plastic on the snare side only.

The snares are directly responsible for the individual tone of a side drum. They consist of a series of wire, wire-covered silk, or gut strands which lie across the lower head. Eight or more strands are advised. They must lie evenly on the drumhead and be adjusted to produce a crisp sound. If the snares are too tight the tone of the drum is choked. An instant (and silent) snare release is essential, as it makes possible a quick change to side drum without snares, and certain improvisations such as substitution for tenor drum. Also the release of the snares when the instrument is not in use obviates the otherwise distressing snare buzz set in motion by nearby instruments.

An adjustable tone control damper (internal for preference) adds to the utility of a side drum as it allows resonance to be reduced to a minimum. A soft duster placed on part of the drumhead will also relieve undue 'ring' and assist a *ppp* if desired.

The stand for the side drum must be solid and have ample adjustment for height and rake.

Maintenance of the side drum should include periodical dismantling of the counter hoops to remove the dust and fluff which collect between the hoop and the heads. The heads can be cleaned with a damp cloth, but must dry out before use.

They should remain tensioned when the instrument is not in use. If for reason of adverse atmospheric conditions tension is added to a calf head, the pressure should be reduced again after use in case of change of temperature. A spot of oil on all working parts, including those on the side drum stand, is recommended.

Side drum sticks

The sticks for the side drum are made of various woods. The five woods most commonly used are hickory, lancewood, ebony, rosewood, and beech. Hickory sticks are the toughest and are advised for all-round .purposes. When choosing a pair of sticks, it is important to see that they are even in length, weight, and balance, and that they both produce the same note from an object such as woodblock, table or desk. Test for straightness by rolling them along a flat surface. If the tip goes up and down, the stick is bent and will prove troublesome.

The length of the average side drum stick is approximately 15½ in.; the weight varies with the class of wood and ranges from 1¼ to 2½ oz. A taper of about 3½ in. in length is recommended, as this measurement ensures a stoutish stick which will stand up to hard work in the forte passages, and also produce the correct tone of the drum at piano level. Change the weight of the sticks as little as possible: wherever practicable obtain varying dynamics by technical approach.

The grip

There are two accepted methods of holding side drum sticks: the 'traditional' grip used when the drum is played at an angle; and the 'matched' grip, generally used when the drum is played horizontally. Figs. 2-5 illustrate the traditional grip. In this grip the left hand is held with the palm facing upwards. The stick is firmly gripped in the crutch of the thumb and first finger at a point governed by the length and weight of the stick (normally one quarter of its length). It rests lightly on the middle joint of the third finger which acts as a cushion. The first and second fingers control with a light pressure or release, according to style. (This grip is known as the rabbit grip, so called from the silhouette of the hand.) The right hand is held with the palm facing downwards. The stick is gripped between the fleshy part of the thumb and the first joint of the index finger. (Though the sticks are firmly gripped, the wrist muscles must be completely relaxed.)

In the matched grip both sticks are held as the right hand stick in the traditional grip (Figs. 4 and 5).

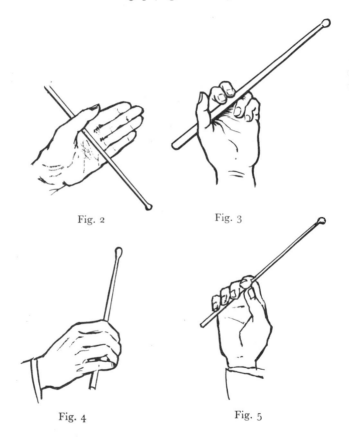

Fig. 2

Fig. 3

Fig. 4

Fig. 5

Height and angle

The playing position of the side drum is governed by several factors. The average professional positions the side drum at about hip height, whether standing or sitting; this position allowing the sticks to 'fall' comfortably on the drum. Though no hard and fast rule can be laid down, an angle of about 45 degrees is customary for orchestral playing. In modern-style drumming the side drum is played horizontally, to accommodate a special technique, and to allow for rapid changing to cymbals, tom-toms, etc. (This position is adopted by certain orchestral players.)

The playing of the side drum at an angle is a relic of the instrument's use for marching purposes. For generations this position has been used in orchestral performance, in the main by players who have had youthful experience of the 'leg' drum, or who have been taught by those with this experience. Since the present-day conditions demand the 'all-round' percussionist, the tyro may consider it advisable to link the side-drum with the timpani and tuned percussion, and adopt the horizontal position. There are, and may remain, two schools of thought regarding these techniques. Those who favour the drum at an angle contend that it looks and sounds best in this position. Many multi-percussionists however ask: why not one technique?

Striking the drum

The drum is struck in the manner indicated in Figs. 6 and 6a. It should be noted that, whilst the arms are not a-kimbo, they do not grip the sides of the body. The sticks should strike the drum with a direct resounding blow, avoiding any tendency to a circular movement, particularly in the left hand. The muscles of the forearm give power, and the wrist acts as a hinge. Normally no trouble is experienced with the initial movement of the right hand. The left hand can be assisted in the early stages if it is imagined that an accumulation of liquid is being flicked from the first finger.

The subsequent hard work at the rudiments will be made easier if the 'feel' of the drum (or pad) is acquired early on. The first step is to strike the instrument firmly and clearly with the left stick six times, at a speed of one beat each two seconds. Repeat with the right hand, still at a slow tempo, the object being to correct mentally between the beats any fault in the blow. The instrument should be struck in the centre (see the later remarks on side drum tone).

Whilst it is natural to look down at the drum when

practising, this should not become a habit. Keep the eyes looking forward, as this is most necessary when playing from music and watching a conductor.

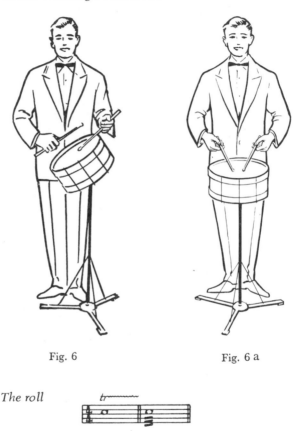

Fig. 6   Fig. 6 a

The roll

The hall-mark of a good performer on the side drum, in addition of course to good musicianship and a perfect sense of rhythm, is the possession of a well-controlled roll. The roll, the technical term for a sustained note or tremolo on all the instruments of percussion, consists of rapidly reiterated beats free of rhythmical stresses. It requires considerable practice to acquire, and constant application to maintain proficiency in this essential element of side drum technique. The legitimate roll (on the *side* drum) is produced by alternate rapid *double* beats known as Dad-dy-Mam-my. The impression of a continuous sound is obtained by steadily accelerating the beats to the required speed — known as closing the roll.

The single beat roll is produced similarly, but by alternate *single* beats, steadily accelerating. A sustained sound can be reasonably achieved in the early stages by making a slight 'press' or buzz on each beat. (As sustained notes on the timpani and tuned percussion are produced by means of the single beat roll, it could be argued that the Dad-dy-Mam-my roll is of small consequence to the all-round percussionist. A good case can be made out for this argument, but it remains true that the legitimate roll, and the dexterity achieved by perfecting it through hard practice, provides a 'sheet anchor'.)

Exercise 1 starts very slowly. (Note the metronome markings. The side drum is indicated, as is usual, in the third space.) Begin by striking the instrument firmly as indicated. Continue the beats at a steady tempo for a period of 1 to 2 minutes. Rest a minute and repeat the exercise with intervals over a period of 15 minutes. The next step is to repeat the formula with a slight increase in tempo. Given two periods of 30 minutes' practice daily, progress will be apparent within a few weeks, and the wrists will become sufficiently supple to deal with further exercises. The wrists get less tired if the practice is spread over two periods.

The effort required to accelerate the beats into a close roll can best be likened to climbing a hill; at a certain point one is conscious of reaching the summit, and the descent on the other side is somewhat easier.

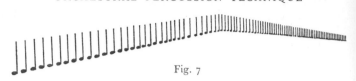

Fig. 7

Ex. 2 will come as a relief if the ascent seems endless. The doubling of the tempo gives a feeling of achievement, whilst any slight 'stagger' in the more rapid beats can be corrected in the slower strokes which follow immediately.

When the wrist action improves through constant practice of the double beat, it will become apparent that the second stroke begins to fall more easily and the sticks bounce readily when the primary blow is well delivered. It then becomes a matter of controlling the rebound of the first and second strokes, and avoiding any possibility of a 'dither' after the second beat. As speed increases, clarity of stroke – particularly in the left hand – should be tested by executing the exercises to date on two differing surfaces – such as a side drum head and the hard side of a practice pad. The separate beats are then readily discerned and any errors revealed.

Stroke rolls

Interest in the double beat exercises can be sustained, during the lengthy process of perfecting the long roll, by studying the shorter and longer 'stroke rolls' – a characteristic of the side drum. The 5, 7, 9, 11, 13, and 15-stroke roll should be practised starting with either hand.

The 6, 8, and 10-stroke rolls are a combination of the 5, 7, and 9 with an added stroke:

L L R R L R
R R L L R L

Usually a 6-stroke roll starts on the pulse beat of the bar, as in Scotch drumming, and a 5-stroke roll *precedes* the beat.

In addition to their value as rudiments, the stroke rolls — particularly the 5, 7, and 9 — can be used in orchestral playing. At a speed of ♩ = 144 it is safe to say a close 5-stroke roll would suit Ex. 8, as indeed it does in the Overture *Pique Dame*. A 7-stroke roll is effective in *Scheherazade* (Ex. 9).

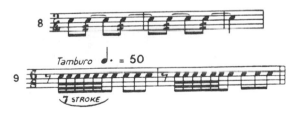

No hard and fast rule can be laid down, as it is obvious that the tempo governs the length of note in all time values. When the pulse is even, a trifling liberty of accent is allowed in the shorter stroke rolls, as it is natural to end these rolls with a crisp stroke. In the main, however, accents should only be used where indicated, and care taken to avoid the bad habit, all too easily acquired, of commencing all rolls with an accent, and finishing them with an ictus: shape can be given perfectly well without undue emphasis.

In the above opening bars of *La Gazza Ladra*, the second bar — which is virtually an echo of the first — can be played near the edge of the drum to help convey the dynamic markings. In the past this method of producing differing volumes would quite possibly have been regarded as incorrect, but modern techniques allow grading of volume by altering the point of striking the vellum. In fact many conductors and players prefer the more silky tone of the side drum when played off centre.

Opinions differ regarding the tied roll. The written tie should be observed in every instance.

On the other hand, it is admissible and convenient to join certain rolls and strokes that are not marked as tied.

Example 12 could be tied if need be. But it cannot be too fully emphasized that the musical pattern must always be appreciated before a join is made.

In Ex. 13 the dynamic marking suggests that the bar be joined.

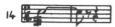

If a tied roll is written finishing on a quaver as in Ex. 14 this is often an indication that a slight accent can be used at the end.

In Ex. 15 (where there is no suggestion of a join musically) it is necessary to carry the roll right to the end of the bar with only a hair's breadth between the two bars (a comma could indicate).

Ornaments

The numerous ornaments are dealt with at length in almost every printed tutor. The three most commonly used in orchestral playing are:

The grace notes of the flam and drag are played lightly in comparison to the main beats, and this effect is best produced by raising the stick playing the main beat higher than the one producing the grace note (or notes). The ruff is played from hand to hand with the accent on the fourth beat, the three grace notes being rapidly executed to avoid delay on the main beat. Grace notes on the side drum are virtually without time value. They are normally written before the bar line, and are invariably played *before* the main beat (see Timpani p.63).

Exx. 19—23 cover normal grace notes.

A liberty is allowed where a succession of grace notes, such as a ruff, may tend to slow the tempo. At brisk march tempo, if the grace notes were played hand-to-hand the result could sound laboured. A 'crush' on the right or left hand, however, would ensure that the main beat is not delayed, and sound in the majority of cases as the composer intended.

The paradiddle

The paradiddle was originally a feature of military drumming. But the orchestral player finds that, besides assisting a good performance on the side drum, it is a veritable port in storm when playing the timpani or tuned percussion. He should accordingly be conversant with the paradiddle in at least four of its forms:

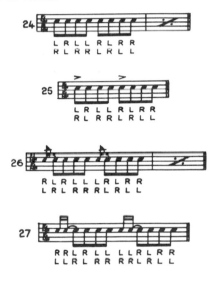

In Ex. 28 a paradiddle (or part of one) can be used to avoid the danger of running into the next bar:

The paradiddle is most helpful when playing 'multiple' percussion. If, for convenience of position, the 'loose' cymbal lies to the right of the side drum, and the previous pattern incorporated a cymbal beat, the obvious method of playing the passage neatly is to commence with the right hand:

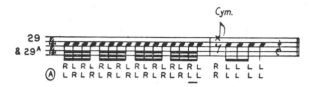

If for any reason this is not possible, a long swing over with the left hand to the cymbal can be avoided by using the paradiddle in the manner shown in the lower row of suggested 'fingerings'. (The cymbal could be damped with the right hand, while the left hand plays the side drum.)

Triplets

The triplet is usually played hand to hand for reasons of smoothness, and to cope with the speed at which reiterated triplets are often encountered.

Care must be taken with groups of six beats. Though it suits the side drum well to play these as two groups of triplets, this phrasing must not be used unless it is so marked. Quite often the six beats are divided into duplets, and it is well to be on good terms, at speed, with the three most usual forms:

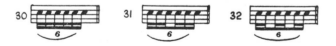

The side drum pattern in Ravel's *Bolero* is interesting. The opening solo, normally played as quietly as possible, is usually played hand-to-hand. The steady crescendo is made by commencing near the rim and moving the sticks gradually towards the centre of the drum. Where two side drummers are employed, as in the full orchestral version, the second side drum enters at bar 289 (same rhythm). Certain conductors require the first few bars to be played with one hand, claiming — maybe rightly — that no two drum sticks produce *exactly*

the same sound. The request of the conductor who demanded the passage to be played in the following style is worthy of consideration and commendation (notice that the pulse falls on the left hand):

L RRR L RRR L L   L RRR L RRR L R R L R R

General remarks

There is no simple solution to the question of 'fingering' the multitude of rhythmic patterns. It is obvious that the number of ways in which a given number of notes can be played is legion. As a general rule, when sight reading or performing works with which one is not well acquainted, the drum is played more confidently if the beats are played singly from hand to hand (except for the tremolo) with occasional use of the paradiddle or double beat. Subsequent study and acquaintance of a work will suggest fingerings which tend to improve performance. For instance, there are numerous ways of executing Ex. 34, but fingerings 4 and 5 can be recommended because the pulse is played each time with the same stick in the same position on the vellum.

R L L R L L   R L L R L R L
L R R L R R   L R R L R L R
L R L R L R   L R L R L R L
L L R L L R   L L R L R L R
R R L R R L   R R L R L R L

Excluding the tremolo, all beats on a correctly tensioned side drum have the same duration. Thus all four bars in Ex. 35 would sound the same, although they appear to be quite different. The various ways of writing out a passage are not unnecessary, however, for they give the percussionist a clue to the orchestral pattern and assist phrasing.

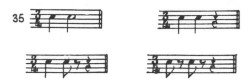

Ex. 36, from the *1812 Overture*, is a typical example of correct writing. The grace notes are played hand to hand (a fraction before the beat) with the quavers and semiquavers sounding as short as possible.

Occasionally it is found helpful to write out an existing percussion part in 'drummer's language'. Here is an example from that gem, Stravinsky's *Histoire du Soldat*.

In orchestral performance the 'lead' should come equally from either hand. In the old-time double-drumming, however, the left hand invariably led. Prior to the invention or general use of the foot pedal on the bass drum, the side drum, bass drum, and cymbals were operated by the 'trap drummer'. The bass drum was to the right of the performer, the side drum immediately in front, and the foot cymbals to the left (see Fig. 8). Ex. 39—41 will illustrate the sort of figures the 'trap dummer' could play. Experts achieved the majority of the grace notes, and the roll was smooth with no 'break' when the bass drum was struck.

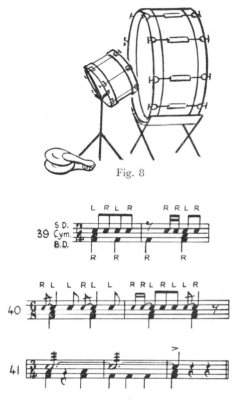

Fig. 8

Though modern conditions rarely call for the arrangement just described, on occasions the trap drummer's technique proves useful. The percussion part of Britten's opera *The Turn of the Screw*, which requires six timpani (including two pedal timpani), bass drum, side drum, tenor drum, cymbals, tam-tam, chimes, etc., calls for the bass drum to be well to the right (out of reach of the foot), as the seating position is governed by the need for access to the pedal timpani.

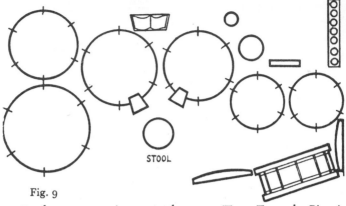

Fig. 9

In the accompaniment to the song, 'Tom, Tom, the Piper's Son' Ex. 42 (from *The Turn of the Screw*) the score calls for a

dry, **hard** tone from the bass drum and timpani (played with the side drum sticks) to match the side and tenor drum. Thus a foot pedal for the bass drum would here be unsuitable, as well as inaccessible.

For normal orchestral purposes the 'one-performer' arrangement shown in Fig. 10 is to be recommended.

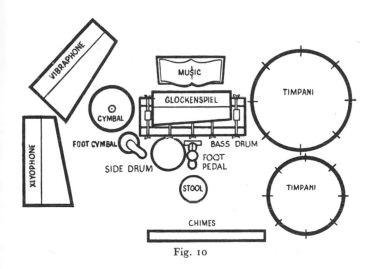

Fig. 10

Of the works mentioned in the Appendix, a close study of the side drum part in the Nielsen Clarinet Concerto and the Geigy Concerto for Basle Trommel by Liebermann would be rewarding. These concertos are formidable and a real study:

THE TENOR DRUM

FR. *CAISSE ROULANTE;* GER. *RÜHRTROMMEL;*
IT. *TAMBURO RULLANTE*

In the orchestra, the technique for this instrument is similar to that for the side drum. Unless otherwise indicated, it is played with side drum sticks, not the felt-headed sticks used in the military band. In place of the regulation tenor drum one can use a deep military pattern side drum without snares, or, in an extremity, the orchestral side drum with snares released. In the majority of cases a funereal sound is required in which case the tone of the tenor drum should be midway between that of the side drum (unsnared) and the bass drum. The modern instrument is rod-tensioned, a method of tensioning now applied to regimental tenor and bass drums.

THE BASS DRUM

FR. *GROSSE CAISSE;* GER. *GROSSE TROMMEL;*
IT. *GRAN CASSA*

Affectionately known as the big drum, this instrument should not belie its name in sound or size. The pitch of the orchestral bass drum should, therefore, be as indefinite as possible, and its diameter (a minimum of 28 in.), sufficiently large to guarantee a deep sound from a correctly-tensioned vellum. Heads of calf-skin or plastic material are equally suitable.

The large single-headed gong drum has a superb tone, but on occasions seems to sound definite in pitch. The individual tone of the full-sized double-skinned bass drum with vellums tensioned slightly differently gives an impression of great depth, resonance, and absence of pitch. A double-ended lamb's-wool beater (tampon), a pair of soft-ended timpani sticks, and a pair of hard felt beaters are essential, together with a clip for fixing a cymbal should it be necessary for the player to play these also.

The bass drum is normally struck with a glancing blow mid-way between the centre and the rim. The beater is held in the right hand, whilst the left hand assists in controlling the length of the note (Fig. 11) by stopping the vibrations where necessary (the fingers of the right hand also participate in this important function). (See below.)

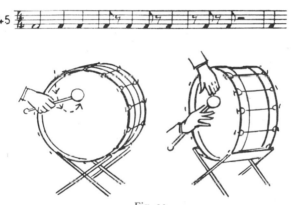

Fig. 11

The tremolo is produced by a single stroke roll with two beaters, or by manipulating the double-ended beater. Where a succession of short notes is required, particularly in rhythmical passages, as in Ex. 46, the instrument should be struck in or near the centre to minimize the resonance.

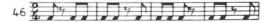

A great moment for the bass drum occurs in the Verdi *Requiem*, where it is customary to use the largest drum available. Stravinsky wrote an interesting and by no means simple part for the bass drum in *The Rite of Spring*.

Where one performer plays both bass drum and cymbals, the cymbal fixed to the bass drum is struck with a held cymbal, military band fashion. It is an advantage when playing short notes if the held cymbal is slightly smaller in diameter than the fixed cymbal. It must be noted, however, that the held cymbal must be of good quality, as it is used quite often for a 'loose' cymbal, being struck with the bass drum stick.

(The bottom space of the stave is generally used for the notes played on the bass drum and the second space for the tenor drum. Strictly speaking, the side drum, tenor drum, cymbals and other small percussion instruments of indefinite pitch, require no clef.)

Bass drum and cymbals combined are occasionally indicated ♩

THE CYMBALS

FR. *CYMBALES*; GER. *BECKEN*; IT. *PIATTI*

A first-class cymbal player is an asset to any orchestra, and so are good cymbals. A pair of cymbals from 15 in. to 18 in. in

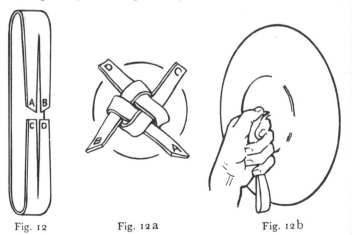

Fig. 12   Fig. 12a   Fig. 12b

diameter will prove adequate for most purposes, but smaller or larger cymbals are more suitable in certain circumstances.

The cymbal straps should be of strong but pliable leather, not less than 1 in. in width, and the cymbal should be insulated from the fingers by means of a felt or leather disc. The strap passes through the central hole in the cymbal and is secured by means of a sailor's knot inside the dome. First shape and letter the ends as in Fig. 12. Then pass the ends through the insulating disc and the hole in the cymbal, and (ideally) through a small leather washer inside the dome. Now fold over A and D (inside B and C). Pass B over D and under A. Hold in position whilst passing C over A and under D as in Fig. 12a. Tighten gradually. The strap is held between the thumb and first finger as illustrated in Fig. 12b.

The cymbals (which are held vertically or at a chosen sloping angle) are 'clashed' with a swift up-and-down or across movement. The full circumference of each plate must meet simultaneously as each crosses with a glancing blow. Long notes on the cymbals are indicated by the terms 'Let ring' and 'Laissez vib'. In this case, the instruments are clashed and allowed to ring freely.

Fig. 13

Shorter notes are obtained by 'damping' the cymbals at the given point by drawing them into the clothes, thus immediately stopping the vibrations. (Use Ex. 47 as an exercise.)

Tchaikovsky, Romeo and Juliet

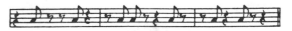

For a series of short notes it is advisable to keep one cymbal as still as possible and near to the body, thereby minimizing the amount of movement needed for 'damping' purposes. The terms 'short', 'stop', or 'sec' are used to signify short notes on the cymbals.

Where a short metallic sound is required, the cymbals can be closed directly on each other and held taut. Occasionally to create a *sustained* metallic sound cymbals are rubbed together or the edges rattled (two-plate roll).

One of a pair of cymbals can be held and a tremolo produced by a series of rapid single strokes performed with the free hand, or with reiterating beats, with two beaters held four hammer grip fashion (see p. 75): a tremolo with a wire brush is similarly obtained. It is more usual, however, to use a 'loose' cymbal mounted on a stand. This gives the choice of a thinner cymbal than one of the normal pair.

Unless indicated otherwise, soft sticks are used for the roll on the 'loose' or suspended cymbal.

In cymbal playing the professional approach is to alter the dynamics by varying the strength of the blow, though on occasions the edges of the cymbals can be touched for a particularly quiet sound:

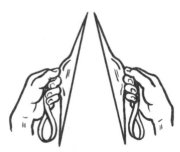

Fig. 14

Cymbals smaller than 15 in. in diameter are an advantage where a 'small' and delicate sound is required, as the tone from a pair of small cymbals played quietly is more silvery than a larger pair struck with the same weight.

·In orchestral music, cymbals are either given a separate part·

or the upper part of the stave. Unless otherwise indicated 'cymbals' applies to a pair (clashed) — sometimes indicated *naturale*, a2, or ⟨ ⟩·

The ancient cymbals (Crotales) — used particularly by French composers: e.g. Berlioz in his *Dramatic Symphony 'Roméo et Juliette'*, Debussy in *L'après-midi d'un faune*, and Ravel in *Daphnis and Chloe* — have a definite pitch:

The instruments are from 2 to 4 in. in diameter and are now manufactured in chromatic sets.

THE TAM-TAM (GONG)

This instrument must be sufficiently large to produce a low note devoid of pitch, whether struck pianissimo or otherwise. A heavy but soft beater is essential. This should strike the gong a glancing blow a little off centre. Where possible it is advisable to lightly vibrate ('warm up') a tam-tam prior to striking it.

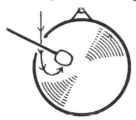

Fig. 15

Unless a small gong is requested it is ruinous to the score to attempt to substitute one for the tam-tam. In such masterpieces as the 'Pathétique' Symphony and *The Dream of Gerontius* it is better to use a large cymbal. Certain Asiatic (bossed) gongs have definite pitch, and are required at times to conform with operatic and symphonic scores. (Tuned gongs are now produced in Europe with a compass up to four chromatic octaves.) A *large* Burmese gong gives the effect of a deep-toned bell. (Fig. 16).

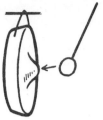

Fig. 16

THE TRIANGLE

The importance of a good technique on the small percussion instruments cannot be overestimated. The quality of the instruments themselves must also be excellent. This is particularly true in the case of the triangle.

Of the various methods of suspending the triangle, many professional players favour a holder made from a paper clip:

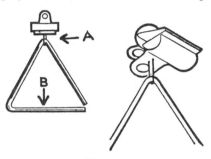

Fig. 17

This simple holder has several advantages. If the loop (preferably fine gut) is sufficiently small to allow the minimum clearance, the instrument will not swing round when struck repeatedly. Also the instrument can either be held for playing purposes, or be clipped to the music stand during long rests. This latter position may be needed if for reasons of 'clean' playing two beaters are necessary, or if the performer is engaged with additional instruments.

The best tone is produced by striking the triangle on the outer side near the top corner: (A) for *pp*; (B) for *ff*.

The sides of ideal instruments measure from 6 ins. to 9 ins.

The tremolo is normally produced by placing the beater (a steel rod about the size of a 6 in. nail) inside the triangle, and moving the beater rapidly from side to side. A quiet tremolo is best played inside the top corner. The beater can be lowered for a crescendo. Grace notes or rapid passages can be played with one hand if the beater is moved inside the triangle from left to right, or from right to left.

Composers indicate when the triangle is to be struck with the side drum stick. In the original version of *Façade*, Walton obtained a curious bell-like sound by having a suspended cymbal struck on the edge with a triangle.

THE TAMBOURINE

FR. *TAMBOUR DE BASQUE;* GER. *SCHELLENTROMMEL*
IT. *TAMBURINO*

The diameter of the orchestral tambourine should not exceed 10 in. as a larger instrument tends to prove cumbersome. Ten pairs of jingles are necessary. The tambourine is struck on the vellum with the fingers, knuckles, or palm of the hand, or on the knee, according to the volume of sound required. A tremolo is obtained by shaking the instrument with a deft turn or turns of the wrist. The thumb roll is an interesting feature of the tambourine; it is indicated by the phrase 'with the thumb', though it is permissible to use the thumb where *not* indicated, if an extremely quiet tremolo is required. Briefly, the thumb roll is a means of vibrating the jingles by friction on the vellum. The pad of the thumb is first moistened with the tongue or damp sponge, and then rubbed with the forefinger to render 'tacky'. The thumb is then rubbed round the edge of the vellum with a gentle pressure. Practice will produce thumb rolls of increasing lengths, though one is limited, obviously, by the circumference of the instrument.

For rapid passages, the tambourine can be played with two hands, or placed between the hand and knee, as shown in Fig. 18. Note that the tambourine is moved downwards to strike the knee, and upwards to strike the hand, performing the following and similar examples in the manner directed in Ex. 49.

Fig. 18

When the tambourine is played with two hands, it is customary to place the instrument on the knees or on a cushion, vellum downwards, and strike the rim of the tambourine with the tips of the fingers, or, as is sometimes requested, the drum sticks.

Ex. 50 embraces the points so far discussed, and would seem to cover the majority of orchestral examples. On rare occasions, one can use *two* tambourines, one in each hand, played on the knees. This suits rapid passages that have to be played double forte.

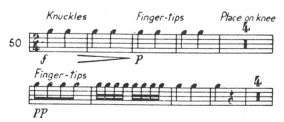

Maintenance on the tambourine should include an eye to the pins upon which the jingles are mounted, as these have a tendency to work loose. A slack vellum will tighten if soaked with a wet cloth and allowed to dry out slowly.

THE CASTANETS

The orchestral percussion player can seldom imitate the superb artistry and technique of the Spanish castanet player, if only because it is not possible (or rarely so) in orchestral practice to affix the castanets to the thumb in the traditional style.

The handle-type castanets are, however, adequate for orchestral playing, and are well suited to the normal percussion technique. Certain beats are produced by tapping the castanets (held in the right or left hand as desired) on the knee or palm of the hand, or shaking in the air with a flicking movement.

The castanets are shaken for a tremolo. They can be held in three positions: upwards, straight out, or pointing downwards, the latter position being the best position for the quiet roll (this applies also to the tambourine). Of the various means of executing rhythmic patterns, the best method of performing the rhythms in Ex. 51, and those like them, is to hold the instrument horizontally in the least deft hand, with the forefinger pressing lightly on the upper blade, as in Fig. 19.

Fig. 19

The lower blade is then struck lightly with the fingertips of the other hand, or strummed in the Spanish fashion. The latter method is best likened to strumming with the fingers whilst cogitating. Alternatively, the blades of the castanets can be secured in an open position with the finger and thumb, and moved between the open fingers and thumb of the opposite hand, as in Fig. 20.

Fig. 20

Two pairs of castanets are helpful to overcome certain difficulties, but they should be well-matched. In a quiet passage the top blades can be held down with the forefingers so that only the bottom blades click, thus ensuring clarity. Or the two blades may be secured to a block of hard wood by elastic or spring steel, and played with the fingers.

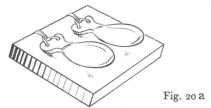

Fig. 20 a

Given proficiency on the triangle, tambourine, and castanets, the remaining small percussion instruments present no serious problems.

THE TIMPANI (It.)

The orchestral kettledrum consists of a copper bowl, with a vellum stretched over the top of it. The vellum is lapped round a hoop (the 'flesh hoop'), variably tensioned by means of pressure on a counter hoop through the medium of threaded tuning handles or other mechanism. A range of at least a perfect fifth is possible on each drum. The diameter of the bowl determines the basic pitch of each kettledrum — the larger the bowl the lower the pitch.[1]

Of the percussion instruments, the timpani are the most noble and possibly the most satisfying to play. In symphonic circles they are referred to apart from the percussion; in fact, it is not etiquette to call the timpanist a percussion player at all. Despite this tradition, however, it is obvious the timpani are instruments of percussion. (Not that it is the writer's purpose to lower the kettledrummer from his exalted and deserved pedestal. Moreover, the traditional term — 'timpani and percussion' — has many advantages. For instance, it is a great help at rehearsals when directions are being given to the different sections.)

Over 250 years ago composers of the calibre of Purcell realized the possibilities of the cavalry kettledrums as orchestral instruments, and introduced them into compositions. In two-and-a-half centuries, the instruments have developed from the cavalry type kettledrum with its slow and laborious means of tuning, to the present-day machine drum which has a pedal tuning mechanism. Contemporary composers are taking great advantage of the new types of timpani. The result is that the timpanist's task has by no means lessened with the instrument's improvement. On the contrary, the modern trend makes increasing demands on the player of today.

The essentials of an orchestral timpanist are: an unerring sense of rhythm, an accurate sense of pitch, the ability to

[1] Fibre-glass bowls have proved successful. Though slightly less resonant than copper, they are durable and light in comparison (and are cheaper). They are applied to pedal and hand-tuned timpani.

produce a good 'tone', and, not least, a desire to hold a position of responsibility. The aspiring timpanist should consider well whether he possesses, or can acquire, a good sense of rhythm, coupled with a good sense of perfect or relative pitch. One still meets with instances of the musical 'failure' being given the chance to study percussion. If the reason for such failure is the inability to grasp the complications of figuration, or a poor sense of rhythm, or a sense of pitch so vague that he cannot even sing or whistle anywhere near the true note, then a professional standard is beyond him, and his music making must be done in circles where the demands are less.

The student who possesses the right qualifications should begin his study by gaining access to a pair or a set of three timpani. Though it is possible to practise stick manipulation, reading, and the like on practice pads, certain work in the way of 'feel', tone production, and tuning must be done on the instruments themselves even in the early stages.

Heads

The heads for the timpani are as important as the construction of the shell. Though there is an ever-increasing use of the plastic head, it would be unwise to omit reference to the use and manipulation of calf skins. When choosing a calf head, see that it is even all the way round, and that the backbone is central. A fair test for even thickness – at least round the edges – can be made with the thumb and forefinger, or a micrometer. Transparency is not by any means always a guide to quality or thickness. Quite often what appears upon examination to be an excellent vellum may prove unsuccessful on the drum. Little can be done with a poor skin, though it should be noted that dissatisfaction with vellums is quite often due to a slightly 'egg-shaped' bowl.

Well-prepared skins vary from 7 to 12 thousandths of an inch in thickness. A head that is too thick tends to be tubby and lacks resonance. On the other hand a reasonably stout vellum will stand up to hard work, and is of advantage if the drums are subject to misuse in any way. The heads should vary in thickness with their size. For general purposes, a set of three timpani are best equipped with heads 10, 8½, and 7 thousandths of an inch in thickness, with the thinnest skin on the smallest drum, although the inconsistency of the calf vellum makes it difficult to establish a golden rule in this respect.

Considerable progress has been made with plastic timpani heads. As with the side drum, the calf skin and plastic head have their respective advantages, and where both are available are a matter of personal choice. The plastic head is virtually unaffected by atmospheric conditions. Its durability (and price) suggests that it may be useful where the drums are subject to hard treatment. The calf head has indisputable qualities, and most professionals agree that it has a more singing tone. All plastic heads are machine lapped to suit floating head counter hoops only.

The plastic head is supplied ready mounted cemented to aluminium. The cementing process is complicated and difficulty may be experienced in equipping the older type drums with plastic heads.

Lapping and upkeep

The calf head is secured to the square or oblong flesh hoop by a process known as lapping. Acquaintance with this simple process is interesting and useful. First make certain that the flesh hoop fits the shell correctly. A wooden hoop should have just sufficient clearance to allow free movement when the vellum is mounted. If the hoop is larger than the required size it tends to curl under constant pressure. (A curled hoop can be rectified to a great extent if it is turned over when relapping.) Floating heads are fitted to metal hoops which should fit in the sectioned counter hoop with sufficient clearance to allow at least two thicknesses of vellum. Metal hoops should be plated to prevent rusting. Cadmium plating is preferable as the more glossy chromium offers less grip.

The diameter of the vellum should be at least 4 in. larger than the outer measurement of the flesh hoop, the exact size of the vellum being governed by the size of the flesh hoop section. A wood hoop should not be less than $3/8$ in. thick by $1/2$ in. deep, or $5/16$ in. thick by $7/16$ in. deep. Metal hoops are a little smaller.

To mount the vellum. It is first soaked in cool water (not more than 65° F.). Five minutes' soaking will usually render the vellum soft and pliable, though in the case of a relap the hardened edges require a good deal more time and plenty of manipulation with the fingers and thumb. When the head has been soaked for the proper amount of time, it is then spread out on a large table (a glass or other shiny-topped table is ideal), and all surplus water removed from both sides by mopping with a soft cloth. Unless the head is to be double-lapped on a steel hoop, it is placed with the smoothest side (the beating side) face downwards.

To ensure the necessary slack in the head, a wooden bowl or large soup plate should be placed under the centre of the vellum. The hoop is then placed centrally on the vellum, and any necessary reduction in size made by scissoring round the edge, remembering that a backbone slightly out of centre can be corrected if the head has a surplus. The lapping is now started with the aid of a standard lapping tool or a rounded spoon handle. Fold a small portion of the head neatly over and under the flesh hoop, tucking it gently in with the lapping tool. It is advisable to tuck opposite sides by dividing the hoop in four equal parts, and then continue the remainder in like manner until the operation is complete, using small wooden clothes pegs to hold the lapping in position if it proves refractory. On no account pull the hoop out of round, as an egg-shaped vellum will be troublesome and will even tend to pull the bowl out of shape unless this is heavily reinforced. If possible, move round the table yourself when lapping rather than move the vellum repeatedly. A further mopping of the vellum and cleaning of the lapping tool completes the lapping.

The whole of the vellum must be carefully examined before it is placed on the bowl. The rim of the latter should be examined, any roughness being removed with fine emery cloth, and then rubbed with a piece of paraffin wax. Place the head smooth side upwards on the kettle, with the desired playing position in line with the threaded lug in which the square-topped or loose handle fits. The lug referred to, and the equivalent bracket on the counter hoop, are usually marked, or else the fittings are numbered. The best playing position on the vellum is a matter of trial and error, but a spot an inch or so to the side of the backbone and near to the more opaque part of the head — approximately 3 in. from the rim — will usually give the best results.

Next, attach the counter hoop and screws, and adjust until

a collar ¼ in. deep is obtained. This collar is necessary to compensate for shrinkage as the vellum 'dries out'. If the counter hoop is inclined to rust, blotting paper should be placed between the hoop and the vellum, and removed when the head has dried off.

Place the drum in a cool place for at least thirty-six hours. Its condition must be thoroughly tested before applying further pressure prior to use.

The 'double-lap' applies to floating heads only. The head is lapped with the rough side to the table, and placed on the kettle with the smooth side upward. (The heads on the side and bass drum are lapped in the same manner as the timpani, though of course the wooden bowl should be omitted when lapping a side drum head, as this vellum needs to be lapped as tight as possible. Plastic heads for the side drum are supplied ready-mounted on hoop.)

For protection purposes, strong wooden covers which cover the vellum and handle mechanism are to be recommended. Failing this, discs of five-ply wood with felt glued to the side which faces the vellum prove an excellent protection. Care should be taken to see that the threaded handles are kept well oiled, particularly around and underneath the top washer. There should also be sufficient paraffin wax round the rim and inside the edge of the vellum. A soiled head can be 'washed' with a damp cloth. If for any reason a head has to be removed, it must be slightly wetted on replacement. A short slit can be checked by making a small hole at the extreme ends of the tear with a hot needle, and further repaired with a well-glued patch of vellum.

When the drums are not in use, it is advisable to keep a certain amount of tension on the vellums, firstly to retain the collar and secondly to strengthen the head in case of accident. Each drum should be tuned to the middle note of its range. *If calf heads are left slack in a normal atmosphere shrinkage takes place, and it becomes impossible to obtain the lowest notes.* To save an immediate relap, a head that has become unduly slack through constant hard pressure in damp atmospheres can be tightened a good deal if it is taken off and soaked, or thoroughly slackened and given a good mopping with a wet cloth. Make certain the extreme edge is mopped dry, as moisture near the counter hoop can be disastrous.

The sticks

A variety of sticks is necessary to produce different tone qualities from the kettledrum, and the player should be equipped with at least four pairs: soft, medium, and hard felt, and 'wooden-ended'.

Stiff shafts of cane or hickory are considered the best and are commonly used. They should be approximately 14 in. long and from ¼ in. to ⅜ in. in thickness. An important feature of the timpani stick is its weight. On no account should heavy-ended sticks be used, as apart from being clumsy they tend to produce a 'dubby' tone. An ideal stick is one with a core of balsa wood or cork, covered with piano felt. The cores can vary in size and the felt in thickness. But in every instance the felt must be firmly and seamlessly secured to the core, preferably by stitching as indicated in Fig. 21:

Fig. 21

If the felt is loose on the core the stick will tend to be spongy, and this should be avoided, as the blow and the sound must be simultaneous, which is not possible if there is the slightest 'give' between felt and core.

To complete the stick, small ferrules of wood or rubber should be fixed to the unfinished end. These assist the balance and act as a stop should the handle tend to slip through the fingers. In addition they can be used with the sticks reversed where there is no time to change to hard beaters.

The grip

The sticks are held identically in each hand. The hold is similar to the grip of the right-hand side-drum stick. Figs. 5 and 24 both illustrate the recommended grip. The thumb and index finger grip the shaft, with the second finger acting as a cushion. The second and third fingers are held close in, strengthening the hold for heavy playing. The little finger must always remain clear of the shaft, as pressure with the thumb and *all* fingers tends to hamper the wrist action. The thumbnail should point upwards. The shaft should be held below the point of balance, this latter position being found by laying the stick across the forefinger:

Fig. 22

A stiff cane handle 14 in. long, with a medium-weight head, normally balances approximately 1 in. off centre towards the head. The most convenient place for gripping the shaft is usually 1 in. to 2 in. below the point of balance. A position nearer the butt would tend to make the sticks feel heavy and difficult to handle, particularly in light passages. Conversely, if the sticks are held too near the head they feel light, and heavy passages become hard work.

Playing position and general approach

Whether to sit or stand whilst playing the timpani is a matter of personal choice. A seated position is the most used in the profession (with one or two notable exceptions), and in view of the increased use of pedal timpani is advised.

The best seat is a swivel stool, adjustable in height and with a short back-rest. The stool should be a few inches lower than hip height, and the timpani a similar number of inches *above* hip height; this will give the most comfortable position. The seat should be sufficiently near the timpani to give access to all tuning handles, and yet allow the freedom required to avoid cramp in the arms whilst playing.

The drums are arranged approximately on the circumference of a circle, with the larger drum to the left.

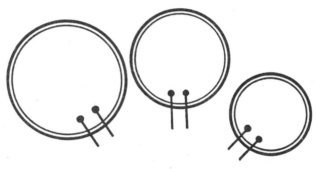

Fig. 23

(Most Continental players perform with the large drum on the right — a relic no doubt of the original cavalry mounting. They claim that this arrangement is easier for playing.) If for no other reason, however, than an acquaintance with the piano keyboard, the xylophone, etc., the normal 'set-up' (large drum on the left) has its merits.

A slight tilt on each drum, upwards away from the player, reduces the danger of the sticks fouling the counter hoop, and raises the back handles to a convenient position. The tilt should be only a few degrees, as more than this causes trouble if the sticks are laid on the vellum whilst tuning, or during a tacet period. The square top handle on hand-screw drums or 'drop' handle is optional. Many players have discarded these fittings in favour of a permanent T-handle, prompted to a certain extent by the rapid changes required in contemporary music. The theory that the vellum is more securely braced near the tuning handles and should be struck there still holds good. But with the introduction of the rigid-sectioned counter hoop the tone *between* the handles is considered equally satisfactory. This latter position is more convenient, and is therefore recommended.

If the timpani and the stool are placed at approximately the height suggested, little difficulty will be experienced in striking the drum in the correct manner, namely with the shaft in the horizontal position, or rather as parallel with the drum head as is possible, allowing the minimum of angle to clear the rim. It will be obvious that if the seated position is unduly high or low, the arms would need to be raised or lowered at an uncomfortable angle to keep the stick horizontal.

Now that the correct striking position and posture have been determined, the all-important approach to the drum can be made. First place a reasonable amount of tension on the head with the tuning handles or pedal. Settle the head by placing the open palm on the centre of the vellum and pressing down firmly. Now rest the stick on the drum head at the playing spot. The shaft is gripped firmly between the thumb and first finger only (the remaining fingers are just clear of the shaft at this moment). Raise the stick upwards with the wrist, at the same time moving the second, third, and fourth fingers away from the shaft (Fig. 24).

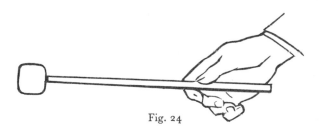
Fig. 24

Again (with the wrist) move the stick downwards towards the drum, closing the second, third, and fourth fingers to the shaft with a 'flipping' movement, thus assisting the stick to strike the drum. After this it is withdrawn with a repetition of the first 'raising' movement. The 'strike' and 'release' should be as rapid as possible, as quick as the 'spit of a snake's tongue'. (The slightest delay stifles the tone.)

This rapidity is the first step to achieving a good tone. Practise the stroke alternately with the right and left hands, slowly at first to permit a mental check on possible error.

Once the 'feel' of the drum is established, the student should acquaint his ear with its pitch by first striking the instrument and *then* humming the note that is 'given off'. If this routine is observed on every possible occasion, and particularly when the drums are being prepared for practice purposes, some of the initial problems in tuning will be overcome.

The roll

Facility on the timpani is acquired by way of basic exercises, commencing with the customary approach to the tremolo or long roll. A sustained note is produced on the kettledrum by reiterating single beats (see side drum). The double beat roll (mam-my-dad-dy) used on the side drum is quite out of place where the timpani are concerned. The muffling effect of the double beat roll reduces the resonance of the drums and completely destroys their characteristic quality.

(A practice pad (or pads) or hard cushions can be used for the 'slogging' exercises. Bongos, timbales and rototoms make excellent practice 'timpani' as they can be tuned to musical sounding intervals (see Tuning p. 49).)

The single strokes are accelerated gradually, bearing in mind that regularity and uniformity of tone are more important factors in the initial stages than speed. The tempo is only increased when it is certain that the beats are being delivered correctly, care being taken to see that the sticks reach the same height when coming away from the drum, and strike the instrument with the same weight with the downward blow. In the majority of cases the left hand needs special attention, for it tends to be weaker both in delivery and rebound, and also to 'wander' with a circular movement instead of moving straight up and down.

In Ex. 1 the alternating beats commence with the left hand

and are repeated indefinitely with slight accelerando. (These and all subsequent examples are to be repeated *ad. lib.*)

The same routine, but starting from the right hand, is observed in Ex. 2.

A minimum of half an hour a day should be spent with these first two exercises, though at this stage a little relief and a good deal of encouragement is experienced if a few minutes be devoted to Exercises 3 4.

Although the 'finished' roll on the timpani is by no means as rapid as the average beginner imagines, its speed should produce a continuous sound on the smallest drum tuned to its highest note when played with reasonably hard sticks. The speed of the tremolo is then adjusted to suit the tension of the vellum, as the lower notes require a considerably slower roll than the high notes. Constant practice and practical orchestral experience will decide for the player the varying speeds necessary to keep the vellum vibrating freely at different tensions and pitches.

Rolls of varying weights and differing dynamic markings require different techniques. It will be found that the best tone is usually produced in a piano roll if the drum is struck a little nearer the rim. The best effect in a crescendo roll is obtained if the sticks make a gradual movement from the rim to the normal playing position (previously selected), where the fuller tone increases the crescendo obtained from the greater rise and fall of the sticks. Similarly, a diminuendo roll is best achieved tonally if the diminishing rise and fall of the sticks is further weakened by an inward movement towards the counter hoop.

The vellum is struck in the normal playing position for the forte roll. The increased volume required for *f* or *ff* rolls is obtained by the greater rise and fall of the sticks. No assistance is obtained in *fff* by moving the sticks beyond the selected playing position to the centre; in fact the volume is decreased by the 'tubby' and indefinite tone resulting from further outward movement.

With the increased speed and rise and fall of the sticks necessary to cope with *ff* and *fff* rolls, the striking positions on the vellum may be widened a little to avoid the sticks colliding. For normal playing one or two inches is sufficient.

The technique required in the case of the 'fortepiano' roll is as follows: After an initial blow has been struck at the required forte, a brief wait is made to allow the tone to die away to almost the desired level of piano before the roll is begun. If a fortepiano roll starts immediately after the primary blow has been struck, the result is in the nature of a diminuendo rather than a fortepiano.

It is essential to be able to begin and end the roll with either hand. Dexterity in this direction will subsequently prove profitable, as certain of the exercises and orchestral examples to follow will show. To ensure a clean attack, the initial stroke of the roll should, under normal conditions, be *slightly* stronger than the succeeding strokes. The finishing stroke should be clean, but with little suggestion of an 'ictus' unless indicated. If the finishing stroke of the roll is to be executed sforzando, there must be no time-gap between the penultimate and finishing stroke. On the other hand, if a fresh start is to be made a very small gap should be observed.

Stick manipulation, cross-over beats

The constant hand-to-hand practice required to attain and retain the tremolo prepares the way for the customary exercises for normal stick routine, cross-over beats, and so forth. Alternate beating is the general rule in timpani playing. Considerable ground can be covered with the required practice exercises, if a given pattern is permutated as in the following exercises:

The same pattern at twice the speed:

Exx. 7 and 8 are the same, rhythmically, as Exx. 5 and 6, but are to be played on two drums, incorporating cross-over beating.

If a triplet is added and the exercises applied to three, four, and five drums, the student will overcome a good deal of the customary teething trouble with the cross-over beat.

Passing from one drum to another with a cross-over beat is characteristic of the original spectacular cavalry kettle-drum technique. The orchestral timpanist is permitted a certain grace of action, but his flourishes must be discreet and never to the detriment of the music.

The change from drum to drum with a cross-beat (or otherwise) must be done swiftly and neatly. The stick engaged in the cross-over must be moved immediately after the drum has been struck, crossing the other stick whilst *it* is delivering the blow. For practice purposes, hand-to-hand duplets, triplets, and quadruplets make excellent exercises. The examples quoted should commence at a speed of ♩ = 80 and be practised until they can be rendered neatly at the speed of ♩ = 144.

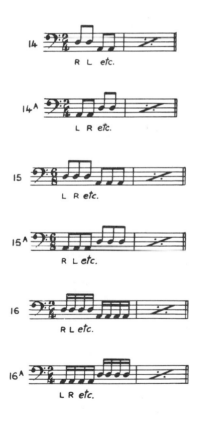

Care must be taken, when making a cross-beat at speed, that the drum stick strikes the drum on the correct playing spot. It is equally important that the impetus adds no strength to the blow. With these points in mind, it is advisable on many occasions to arrange the fingering of a passage in such a manner that a cross-over beat is avoided. Instead of the passage being played consecutively hand-to-hand, a double beat on either the left or right hand is introduced, often in the form of a paradiddle. Try alternative fingering in Exx 11, 12 and 13.

The paradiddle (double beats, etc.)

The paradiddle is a veritable 'port in storm' for the timpanist. Exx. 17, 17a, 18, and 18a, should be practised from a speed of ♩ = 80 to ♩ = 160. They can be extended to four and five drums and permutated as desired.

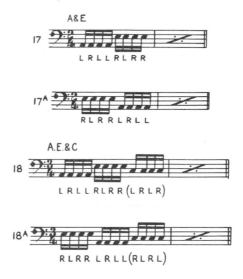

But it is to be remembered that the double beat, paradiddle or otherwise, is only advocated as an expedient, and should not be used indiscriminately to the detriment of a good hand-to-hand technique. A fragment from Delibes' *Lakme* ballet music can be quoted as an example (Ex. 19):

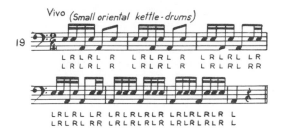

The lower fingering is a poor substitute for the more correct
style above, in which the left hand moves to the top drum
during the brief space afforded by the length of the quaver.

With careful timing and a discreet use of the double beat —
as illustrated in Ex. 20, most passages tend to sort themselves
out.

Good composers, past and present, though often 'handing
out a snorter', e.g. Ex. 20a, rarely present the experienced
player with an impossibility.

Apparently simple-looking passages can 'tie the player up in
knots' unless a double-beat is used here and there. Exx. 21 and
22, played left-right or right-left throughout, would lead to a
display of gymnastics and possible disaster on the first beat of

the second bar (subito *pp*). A double beat with the left hand on the last two semiquavers of the first bar 'irons out' the phrase nicely.

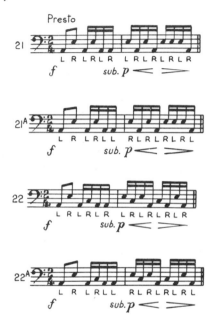

On occasions, even the most accomplished performer is permitted licence in the way of duplicating or altering the position of the drums to accommodate a passage:

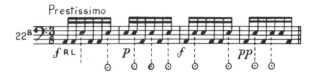

Here a small drum duplicates the E. (See also Beethoven's Eighth Symphony.)

Excellent practice material and considerable food for thought can be found in many standard works from the classical symphonies to compositions of today. Many of the notable examples are quoted in printed tutors.

Tuning

Five full tones are practicable on an orchestral kettledrum (a semitone above or below this compass is *possible*). The normal pair has a compass of an octave from F to F, and the symphonic set of three a range extending from E flat to G:

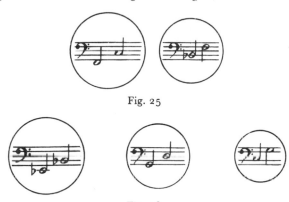

Fig. 25

Fig. 26

A drum 32 in. in diameter is desirable for the occasionally written low D, and small drums (Piccoli Timpani) diminishing from 23 in. are necessary for notes above the top G. The working ranges are shown in the diagrams above, a study of which will show why the dominant is placed above or below the tonic in each instance; for example, with a pair of drums tuned to D and A the dominant note A must be placed on the lower drum as this note is impossible on the smaller drum, and vice versa.

The music for the timpani is written in the bass clef (the instruments sound where written). Composers usually state the notes required at the commencement of the work; e.g. 'Timpani in D, A, and F sharp', or indicate the notes in this manner:

A change of tuning is normally indicated by the words 'Change' or 'Muta'.

The first step in tuning is to get the ear used to the nominal note of the drum. A good deal of practice may be necessary in this respect, as certain of the upper harmonics tend to register quite strongly at first hearing, and are often more audible (even to experienced musicians) than the nominal note.

First place a moderate and even pressure on the drum head with the tensioning screws, and 'settle' the head by gently pressing in the centre with the palm of the hand. The next operation is to even up the tuning. The head should be tapped lightly with the drumstick or finger tip on the playing spot (previously chosen). Next test all round the head with a light stroke at the same distance from the rim, in front of and between each handle, adjusting any recognizable rise or fall in pitch by adding or releasing tension at the required point. With a pedal timpano tune the lowest note on the drum similarly (pedal in initial position).

During this process, difficulty may be experienced in determining the difference between 'pitch' and 'tone' (particularly with a calf skin). The brighter or more 'pingy' *tone* obtained at certain spots must not be confused with sharpness in pitch, nor must the slightly duller-sounding places be considered flat.

When the difference between tone and pitch is confidently recognized, the final adjustments can be made. It may be found that certain places on the head require additional pressure, or the tension reduced to counteract the rise or fall in pitch. (If extra pressure is constantly required at one point, or the drum will not produce a singing tone in spite of repeated attempts to tune evenly, it is possible that the lapping is at fault at or near the most troublesome point.) When the drum produces a steady singing sound, it can be further tested by humming into the playing spot a fifth above the nominal note. The normal method is to bend over the instrument with the head inclined and the lips as near to the vellum as possible.

If the fifth is pitched correctly and the drum is evenly tuned, the response will be quite strong. Thus one can find out whether or not the drum head is producing the required musical note. If necessary the tonic sol-far method can be employed here and on all subsequent occasions.

This interesting experiment can be extended to the full series of harmonics:

with G as the nominal note.

A pair of timpani should now be tuned. The notes D and A are suitable for two reasons; first, the notes are in the middle of the compass of a normal pair of timpani; secondly, the interval of a fourth is characteristic of the kettledrums and gives satisfaction to the ear. A fourth was in fact for some time the only interval used by the early classical composers.

D and A (tonic and dominant of the key of D) are set on a pair of drums with the tonic (D) on the small drum. Begin by releasing most of the pressure from the drum heads. Then proceed to raise the pitch of the drums to the required pitch. No definite formula can be given as to the amount of mechanical movement governing changes of pitch on a hand-screw drum. The amount the handles will need to be turned is determined by the nature of the vellum, atmospheric conditions, and the pitch of the thread of the tuning handles. (Travel on the foot pedal is similarly governed.)

Although a good deal of contention exists regarding the most reliable method to tune hand-screw timpani, the general rule is to begin tuning at opposite handles, and then (if both hands are free) to operate the nearest handles on either side simultaneously, proceeding round the drum in like manner. Constant use of the same drums will accustom a player to the approximate number of turns needed for varying intervals. The amount of pressure on the vellum is also 'felt' through the tuning handles or the foot pedal on pedal-tuned timpani. By these two methods an interval can be judged reasonably accurately.

To return to the tuning in hand. The tonic (D) is tuned first (this procedure should be adopted wherever possible). In the initial stages the required notes can, if necessary, be taken from the piano or similar instrument of fixed pitch such as a glockenspiel or xylophone. The piano is preferable, as the notes can be heard in the correct position in the stave. After the note (D) has been sounded on the fixed-pitch instrument, it should be sung and the small drum tuned to it. Before tuning the lower drum, sing the required note (A), the dominant (the interval of a fourth below being found by the tonic sol-fa method if need be).

The opinion of a musical friend can now be sought. Let the friend listen to the drums from a reasonable distance and make his observations. Now the friend should play the drums whilst the student listens to them from the same distance. A difference of opinion may exist regarding the intonation, but the subsequent debate will be found helpful and interesting, particularly if a tape recorder is available.

Next, lower the drums to C and G. It is advisable to release the drum a little more than is required when tuning down, so that the tuning can be completed by applying pressure to the vellum. If also the skin is pressed in the middle with the palm of the hand after releasing the pressure, trouble resulting from a binding head is greatly reduced.

The drums should now be tuned in fifths, with the dominant *above* the tonic. First tune the large drum to A. When the tonic (A) is well established, the dominant (E) should be sung.

Now tune the small drum to the E. When both drums respond freely when the nominal and fifth are hummed into them, an extremely interesting phenomenon can be experienced. Sound the small drum quite strongly and immediately stop the head vibrating with the palm of the hand. When the intonation is correct, the lower drum will reply by 'singing' the dominant E. This is the result of sympathetic vibration.

Accustom the ear to *all* the fifths (and fourths) which are practicable on a pair of drums by tuning them to the following intervals:

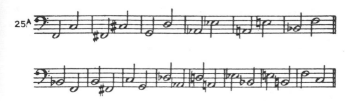

With a normal pair of orchestral drums, only in the keys of B flat and F can the composer place the dominant either above or below the tonic:

With a symphonic set of three timpani the composer has more scope, and the student should become accustomed to the low E and E flat, the high F sharp and G, and the additional fourths and fifths.

All intervals from a semitone to one octave on a pair of drums, and one octave and a third on a set of three, must be practised and listened to with attention. By the time this has been done the ear will become well used to the pitch of the timpani.

In due course there will be little need of recourse to the fixed-pitch instrument. Although *absolute* pitch may 'escape' even the most diligent, certain notes such as A and D will be remembered, and if relative pitch is well established, the occasional use of a tuning fork may be all that is required. (Little trouble is experienced in tuning for the first 'piece' at a rehearsal or performance, as the notes A and D are so easily recognized when the orchestra is tuning up.)

To 'change' and maintain the drums in tune during performance requires considerable orchestral experience. The student should take advantage of every possible occasion to perform with an orchestra, or to sit near and be advised by a professional timpanist during a rehearsal. The task of maintaining pitch during performance can be a nightmare at times. The most disturbing factor (unless the drums are equipped with plastic heads) is that of atmospheric variation, as the tension on a calf skin head is altered immediately and distressingly by changes in temperature and humidity. Both these changes are an enemy of the orchestral kettle drummer. (Eminent players have resorted to electric heating equipment inside the 'kettle' to counteract extreme conditions.)

A moisture-laden atmosphere causes calf heads to lose tension, and consequently the drums flatten in pitch. Wet weather is not the only cause of this, as the air breathed out by the audience in a well-filled hall increases the humidity of the atmosphere in any weather. Either of these conditions, or, as is often the case, a combination of the two, adds a burden to the player, as the drums need constant attention to counteract the fall in pitch. Where possible the final adjustments should be made as near to the entry as possible. Under very bad conditions the top notes will be found particularly difficult and at times actually unobtainable. In such a case the highest note should be played on a smaller drum, if such is available. A spare 22 in. drum is a great help in this respect, as the highest note can be placed on it, leaving the other drums available for notes in the middle or lower part of their range.

If a drum is tuned to its highest note on a wet night, it will in all probability flatten whilst it is being played. There is even the danger of the head 'going' or pulling down to the extent of the need of subsequent relapping.

Where the player is limited to a pair of timpani and the written high F is unobtainable, the tunings can be reversed in the keys of B flat and F.

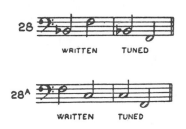

With the set of three drums the written high F, F sharp, or G can be treated similarly. The reverse routine can be applied if an extremely dry atmosphere renders the lower notes impossible. Moisture carrying units are used to rectify.

Conductors are generally aware of the timpanist's task when he is coping with adverse conditions, and give such assistance as the score will allow. It is well to bear in mind that the tension on calf heads must be considerably relaxed after a performance in a damp atmosphere, as a possible change of weather may tighten the skins alarmingly. One needs to be alert to the continual sharpening of the drums in a dry atmosphere. Modern heating, lighting, and air-conditioning, and dry or frosty weather, will keep the timpanist busy counteracting the steady rise in pitch of the drums. As in humid atmospheres, it is advisable to leave the *final* adjustments to the last moment.

The orchestral timpanist

A specimen concert programme including classical and later compositions will give a good opportunity to illustrate the technique of 'tuning' throughout a performance.

This programme requires three hand-screw (or pedal) tuned drums, and will illustrate the timpanist at work.

The timpani must be placed in a position where the conductor is in *full view*, and not seen *through* the players in front, or by means of a periscope. The last-mentioned instrument will become necessary if the double bass players get any taller! (Though this grand section of the strings must be given its due, for the players are most accommodating if requested to move a little to the right or left, and if sufficiently near are most helpful where a 'cue' is concerned, or a note needs to be checked for intonation, etc.) Before commencing a night's work, it is worth while making certain the music stand is secure, and seeing that a rack or small table is at hand upon which to keep the spare sticks.

The concert, being entirely orchestral, begins with the National Anthem in the key of G (the choral version is often in B flat). The notes required are G, D, and C. The large drum is first tuned to the note G (the tonic), one full tone below the A to which the orchestra is busily tuning. The G can be reached by first humming the A and then descending a tone, or two semitones. When the large drum is satisfactorily tuned to G, the top drum should be tuned to D (the dominant a fifth above). The middle drum is now tuned to C (the subdominant), a fourth above the tonic or a tone below the dominant.

D and A are now required for Mozart's Overture to *The Marriage of Figaro*. Given favourable conditions, these notes can be placed either on the small and middle or on the middle and large drums. Having in mind the brilliance of a well-tensioned drum, it is fair to say that the larger drums, at present tuned to C and G, suit the present purpose best, as the overture demands a crisp and crystal-clear tone.

To accommodate the latecomers, and to allow the audience to settle themselves down, cough in comfort, and open and close their programmes a few times without being disturbed by the music, a reasonable wait is normal between the National Anthem and the overture. This allows the timpanist adequate time to make the necessary changes. In the time available it is possible to tune G to A with care; twice round the drum in steps of a semitone or thereabouts is advisable (if hand-screw).

The middle drum is now changed from C to D. The small

drum, being already tuned to D, can be used as a check. If the two drums now tuned to D are sounded together, and a 'beat' is audible, the larger drum needs a slight adjustment either way to achieve unison. As the two instruments will now respond to each other, it is advisable to stop the small drum vibrating by sympathetic resonance during the overture, by placing a cloth or sheet of music on the vellum.

No better example of a symphony could be quoted for our purpose than Beethoven's Eighth, which requires low F, middle C, and top F.

As with the Mozart Overture, only two drums were originally intended, and these would suffice, but with the third drum available an excellent C can be obtained on the middle drum, leaving the small drum 'spare' for the high F.

For tuning purposes, the A at present on the large drum (or again the oboe A) can be used as a 'springboard'. Tune the middle drum to C, arriving at the required note by humming first the note A and then moving up by sol-fa; doh, ray, re. Now change the large drum from G to F, first humming the note G to which the large drum is tuned, and then descending a tone (or two semitones). The final, acid test (referred to earlier) is to hum the C into the F, or strike the middle drum (C) and note if the lower drum (F) 'sings' back the C. No difficulty should be experienced in humming the top F one octave higher than the note on the large drum, or a fourth above the middle C. The small drum can now be tuned. If the octave is perfect, the drums will respond to each other. Time permitting, the position of the small drum can be changed with the middle drum to obviate crossing over the centre drum when playing the octave Fs hand-to-hand in the last movement:

Fig. 27

(See paradiddle, double beats, etc.)

Before leaving the platform for the interval refreshment, it is as well to rearrange the drums (if they have been moved) and condition them, by 'releasing' the top F and middle C and applying a little pressure to the low F.

If the second half of the programme commences with the *Enigma Variations* (a demanding and most rewarding work), it would be helpful to make an early return to the platform so that the drums can be tuned and 'evened-up' in reasonable silence.

The first variation requires the notes, G, B flat, and F.

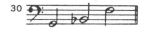

The middle drum is first tuned to B flat; the A for tuning purposes being taken from a tuning fork if need be. The small drum is now tuned to F, a fifth *above* B flat. Finally the large drum is tuned to G, a third *below* the middle drum. (The tonic sol-fa method can be used in these and all subsequent tunings if desired, and needs no further mention.)

At the end of the first variation, as elsewhere, a clear indication is given in the timpani part that certain notes are to be changed. In this instance: F to D, B flat to C sharp. Note Elgar's correctness in instructing the small drum to be changed first, as only G and D are required in the second variation. In the last bar, a pause, the note D is held in the strings and can be 'used' for testing the pitch when changing the small drum. It is often a help in tuning to refresh the ear with a known note, particularly from instruments sounding in the timpani register (horn, trombone, cello, etc.); in fact, if certain tunings prove difficult to pitch the score can be referred to, and pencilled notes made at the required places in the timpani part. In the work now being performed, certain notes can be confirmed from the excellent instrumental cues preceding many of the timpani entries.

There is ample time to change the middle drum (from B flat to C sharp) during the longish rest in the second variation, and the pitch can be tested by gently flicking the vellum with the finger-tip during the final pause bar, at the start of which the cellos and basses play pizzicato G.

The *length* of the notes in Variations 2 and 3 must be observed. To achieve the desired effect, the drums must not sound in the rests which follow. It is obvious that the resonance of a well-tuned kettledrum, if it is correctly struck, will sustain beyond the length of a quaver or crotchet; therefore, the routine of damping must be brought into operation. The vibrations are checked with a deft touch of the flattened, second, third, and fourth fingers of either or both hands (Fig. 28).

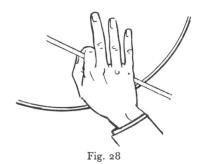

Fig. 28

With practice this action becomes automatic.

(In certain examples to follow, a means of damping is suggested which employs this method. Experience will decide how and when to damp.)

In the first seven bars of Variation 2:

the vibrations can be stopped on the third quaver of each bar with either hand. In bar seven it is better to damp the D with the right hand whilst the left plays the two semi-quavers on the lower drum.

In Variation 3 the notes are sufficiently isolated to allow the damping to be done without effort by the hand not employed in striking the drum:

With the drum tuned to a note well in the upper part of its compass the instrument is more easily controlled, for less damping is required on a strongly-tensioned drum than one tuned to a lower part of its register and therefore slacker.

No pressure must be placed on the vellum when damping, or a slight sharpening of the note will be experienced. In all circumstances, the damping must be inaudible, which is easier said than done. (On certain recordings where a 'close mike' position has been used, the writer has resorted to the use of chamois leather finger-stalls).

In Variation 4, with the drums tuned to C, G, and D, it is advisable to damp the three drums at the end of the second bar:

The vibrations of the small drum should be checked first as it is the last drum of the pattern to be struck, and its vibrations will give additional resonance to the lower G.

(The phenomenon of sympathetic resonance must be continually borne in mind. When the drums are tuned a fifth apart, the lower drum will always vibrate when the higher drum is struck, provided of course that the interval is correct.)

The quaver in the seventh bar is observed by damping at the end of the roll, and the remaining two drums are then also damped, to render them as silent as is possible during the bar's rest that is to follow.[1]

The last twelve bars of Variation 4 can be quoted as one of the almost insurmountable problems facing the timpanist.

Unless pedal drums, ideally equipped with foot operated fine tuners, are used, it is impossible to play in tune the steady crescendo roll. A given tension will not produce the same note over the whole dynamic range, for on a drum tuned to a note below the centre of its compass, as in the present case, the head stretches quite considerably under the weight of a heavy blow. Thus the pitch will flatten steadily (though only slightly) as the crescendo roll continues. It is not possible to give a touch even to the nearest handle during the execution of the roll, so it must be decided whether to have the beginning of the roll sounding fractionally sharp, or the louder rhythmic pattern which follows sounding flat. Of the two evils, the former is in this case the less grievous as the louder passage is heard at greater length, and the average ear tolerates an error above the true note better than one below it. If circumstances had allowed, it would have been an advantage to tune a larger drum to D, as a tight skin holds up better under a *ff*. It is worth remembering that an important solo, whether *ff* or otherwise, should be played on fairly tight vellum.

The crescendo rolls in Variations 5 and 6 and are most important, and there is ample time to tune the small drum to

---

[1] The importance of 'damping' is obvious, if one considers the damaging effect of a drum 'ringing' during the silence following an orchestral tutti.

top G as instructed (D–G high) in the four bars' rest before eighteen, ready for the solo pattern in Variation 7. With a symphonic set of three the 24 in. drum will take the high G comfortably. If pedal drums are being used the standard drum – 23 in. or near – is a perfect size for notes from D to high A. (At a pinch a 25 in. drum with a plastic head will reach high G.)

For the purpose of clarity fairly hard sticks should be used, and a certain amount of damping may be effective. As it is not possible to use the finger damping method in this variation (a veritable *tour de force*) the resonance of the drums can be lessened by placing a soft cloth or felt pad on the vellum. Circular discs of piano felt, graduated from 5 to 7 in. in diameter to suit the different-sized drums, make most effective dampers. If these are secured to the tuning handles with tape, they can be placed where needed. The position of the damper on the vellum controls the 'check'.

With the felt pads placed at the first position the resonance of the drums is moderately controlled.

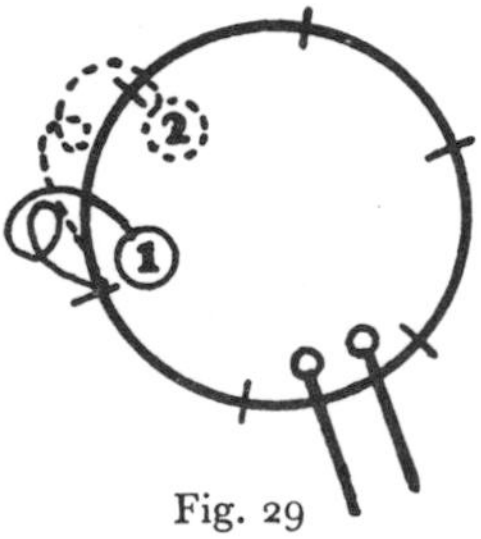

Fig. 29

As the pads are moved to position 2, the length of the note becomes shorter. These damping pads are a useful addition to the timpanist's kit, as they can be used at the discretion of the player, and at all times when instructions are given for the drums to be damped or muted (coperti, sordi, voile, sec, etc.). They are a boon in the case of this variation. If the pads are placed at the position '1' for the commencement of the solo, and it is felt further clarity is required, the position of the pads can be changed after the entry.

It is important to observe the dynamic markings and the

phrasing of the solo figure. If it is read bar by bar and the natural accent *felt* on the first beat of each bar, there is little possibility of the pattern developing a sense of 3/4 rhythm:

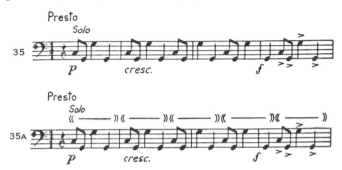

The brief respite in Variation 8 (tacet) is welcome, and a 'breather' can be taken before tuning the drums to the required notes in Variation 9 — E flat, B flat, and low F. The crescendo rolls on the timpani are a feature of this variation, and their performance will be found thrilling and satisfying.

It will be found that the grace notes in Variation 11 are written within the bar:
A glance at the score will make it clear that the ornament must sound a split second ahead of the barline, to ensure the main beat coinciding with the orchestral tutti.

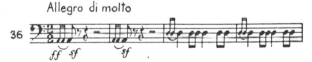

There is little to do in Variation 12, but Variation 13 is of great interest. Elgar's instruction to play the rolls with the side drum sticks is generally disregarded (respectfully) in favour of coins (two ten penny pieces). The tremolo, which must be close and even, should be played near the rim. The change from side drum sticks (or coins) to 'naturale' at the end of the roll suggests either wishful thinking on the part of the great composer, or supreme confidence in the performers of his day. There are various ways to deal with the situation.

One method is to commence the roll using the butt-end of the timpani sticks as side drum sticks, and making the change to soft ends at the *end* of the tremolo. The sticks should be held in the centre of the shaft with the customary grip. The wrists are turned over for the roll, which is played hand to hand with a slight 'buzz' to give the effect of a side drum roll. The roll should be held as long as possible before the change to 'naturale', and the twist over to felt ends should be made swiftly and neatly at the last moment. Alternatively, the roll could be played with the fingernails, or thimbles could be worn; both devices allowing the sticks to be held normally. It is of course possible to grip the coins between the fourth and fifth fingers without greatly disturbing the normal stick hold.

The finale of this superb work contains some high spots for the timpani, and is full of interest for the player.

The final item, Tchaikovsky's Fantasy-Overture *Romeo and Juliet*, requires the drums to be tuned to E, B, and F sharp. The pattern on the timpani adds considerably to the excitement of the percussion in Tchaikovsky's excellent scoring for the duel scene:

The tense heart-beat effect of the triplet rhythm (Ex. 38) (often played with one hand) is enhanced if the drum is slightly muted with the felt damper or the hand.

The last hurdle is the long roll in the final five bars. To accommodate the crescendo from *p* to *ff*, the middle drum should be tuned a fraction on the 'bright' side. It is possible, however, on this occasion to change the larger drum from F sharp to B natural (there is no further need of the lower note).

The four items in the programme have given the timpani (and timpanist) plenty of hard and interesting work, and have permitted the writer to deal with the technique of tuning and damping to the best of his ability.

There are obvious advantages in having two timpani similarly tuned for easing the execution of a difficult passage, or adding to the sonority of a single note or tremolo. But these can be used for other purposes as well, for instance in this example:

It is out of the question to damp the semiquaver in the first bar with the fingers and still approach the roll in the second bar comfortably. If a damping pad were used, it would have to remain on the drum whilst the roll was being played. But two drums tuned to B flat, one of them muted, would simplify this and similar passages.

Additional weight and quality is given to a double forte if the drum is struck with *both* sticks simultaneously. This is indicated thus:

With discretion, a player may use this effect to support other dynamic markings.

Many contemporary works require a minimum of four timpani. The additional instrument proves an asset on numerous other occasions, as it saves many changes and consequent 'ups' and 'downs' on the heads. Manual labour is also reduced. In view of the 122 changes of tuning in *Hiawatha*, this aspect of the timpanist's task is not to be taken lightly. (A good case for pedal drums with tuning gauges.)

Pedal tuned timpani

The pedal tuning drum is by no means a recent innovation. Records speak of a French foot-tuned kettledrum in 1790, and only minor modifications have been made to the excellent Dresden drums made at the end of the last century. There is controversy as to whether the outer mechanism on these and newer models is an advantage, i.e. whether the mechanism fitted inside the bowl of the utility models manufactured in more recent years impairs the tone. Judging by the excellent results obtained on these latter instruments by many professional players, the difference in quality would seem to be small.

Certain models have the advantage of being both hand-screw and pedal operated, whilst others augment the foot tuning with a 'fine-tuning' system. Certain instruments, so-called 'machine drums', are tuned by one handle only. Tuning gauges are a boon in many cases. They must be accurately set and frequently checked, but never used indiscriminately. *Constant resort to tuning gauges leads to a lazy ear.*

Little difficulty is experienced in tuning with the pedal mechanism if proficiency has been acquired with hand-screw drums. The player quickly becomes accustomed to the 'travel' and 'feel' of the pedal. With practice, intervals can be judged reasonably accurately in the first instance. One advantage of pedal tuning timpani is that the counter hoop places tension evenly in one operation. (In many cases square-topped screws replace T handles, giving a clear rim.)

No mechanism exists which allows the drum to be tuned chromatically by a series of steps or notches on the pedal. The reason for this is obviously the inconsistency of the vellum, and the varying degrees of tension required in changing atmospheric conditions. The same conditions render slightly inaccurate the tuning gauges fitted to some pedal timpani, though the assistance quite often afforded by this interesting device cannot be disregarded. The freedom afforded to the hands and the eyes is not the least of the advantages of pedal timpani, in addition to which there is the ability to adjust the pitch of a note at the commencement of a tremolo or while it is being played.

Most modern composers score for the timpani with the machine drums in mind. The changes and glissandi in the

Concerto for Orchestra by Bartók, and his Sonata for Piano
and Percussion, are possible only on pedal tuning drums:

The ascending passage in Strauss's *Elektra* is playable on
pedal drums, as the passage seems to fit very well the natural
downward 'travel' of the foot pedal:

The Variation for timpani in Benjamin Britten's *Nocturne* is
a further instance of careful preparation on the composer's
part. The work calls for four drums, three of which must be
pedal-tuning. The ascending passages are chromatic, and
all start on each drum on the note upon which they have
been halted, thus allowing the player to concentrate upon one
pedal at a time:

Alternative (bars 5 & 6)

The involved tunings and complex figurations found in many modern works present a different picture from the *seemingly* less difficult parts written for the timpani by the early masters. But if for a moment these early works are considered 'a piece of cake', a 'bite' at the Beethoven Ninth will test the teeth and dispel illusion!

The entry of the timpani in the sixteenth bar and onwards is a thrilling experience. Note the tremolo sign indicating a roll (the then prevailing custom). Later we meet the redoubtable demisemiquaver passages, indicated by three strokes through the crotchet — today a method quite often used for writing a tremolo. Played with fairly hard sticks — as in Beethoven's time — the demisemiquavers are recognizable as such. The pattern *must* commence on the right hand to allow the change at the end of the bar. It is interesting to note that the average player would find this passage easier if the drums were arranged in the Continental style, with the large drum to the right hand, and the pattern started with the left hand.

The Scherzo is sufficiently well known to need no comment, but the reader may be reminded of the manner in which Beethoven made use of the two drums struck simultaneously in the fourth movement, and the tuning of the drums in the opera *Fidelio* to the unusual interval of a diminished fifth (A natural and E flat).

Works of composers such as Wagner, Meyerbeer, Tchaikovsky, Berlioz, Sibelius, Stravinsky, and others are sufficiently well quoted in tutors (e.g. those listed in the Appendix) to need no mention here.

Holst gives two players, each on a set of three timpani, some interesting work in *The Planets* suite. Stravinsky's patterns for two timpanists in *The Rite of Spring* are exemplary. Both Bliss and Walton have written magnificent parts for the timpani. Tippett's works are equally challenging. Composers whose works should be studied include Beethoven, Busoni, Bartók, Copland, Britten, Samuel Barber, Hans Werner Henze, and Elliott Carter (see Appendix B).

Finally the student is advised to take every opportunity of hearing experienced players in the flesh — to observe their mode of working, and if possible to receive personal instruction or advice from them. Recent recordings of the major works in which the timpani (and percussion) can be heard to advantage should also be studied.

The respect with which great composers and players regard the kettledrums will eventually be shared by all ambitious students, and they will acquire a deep and lasting affection for these noble instruments.

PERCUSSION INSTRUMENTS
OF DEFINITE PITCH

(THE TUNED PERCUSSION)

Misunderstanding exists regarding the practical requirements of the 'tuned percussion instruments'. It is unfortunate that these instruments are not standardized, at least as far as compass and 'lay-out' are concerned. It is proposed, therefore, at this stage to draw the attention of the amateur to certain features of the glockenspiel, xylophone, etc., which are necessary if they are to conform to present-day demands. (All are classified 'mallet played percussion'.)

The compass quoted in each instance, though not used universally, nevertheless covers the range generally accepted. In all cases the scales are chromatic.

THE GLOCKENSPIEL   (ORCHESTRAL BELLS)

FR. *TIMBRES (JEU DE TIMBRES)*;
GER. *GLOCKENSPIEL;* IT. *CAMPANELLI*

For orchestral purposes the minimum range of the glockenspiel is two and a half octaves:

sounding two octaves higher than here written.

The metal bars vary from 1 in. to 1¼ in. in width, according to the model. Whilst the slight difference in timbre is negligible, the layout of a glockenspiel with 1¼ in. bars renders the 'span' nearer to that of the xylophone. The glockenspiel may have tube resonators. Although this is not usual, the tone of the lower notes of an instrument so equipped is strengthened. This allows the use of softer beaters than are practical on a model without resonators. The piano-action glockenspiel is little used today.

Four types of beaters are essential. 1. Hard (pyraline, ebonite, wood, etc.). 2. Vulcanized rubber. 3. Medium rubber. 4. Soft rubber. The ends (maximum 1 in. in diameter) are best mounted on stiffish handles, which should be 9—12 in. in length. (See 'Four-hammer Playing', page 72.)

THE XYLOPHONE

FR. *XYLOPHONE;* GER. *XYLOPHON;* IT. *SILOFONO*

If it is to be equal to all orchestral and solo purposes, the ideal xylophone should have a range of four octaves ascending from middle C. Three and a half octaves generally cover the normal orchestral requirements:

(sounding as written)

The wooden bars of the modern xylophone are resonated throughout.[1] This strengthens and enriches the sound and makes possible a wide variety of tone colour. In some works, however, such as Saint-Saëns's *Danse macabre*, the resonators could be removed, to ensure a brittle (*bony*) sound.

The two rows of bars may be mounted level, or the back row may be raised. Each method has its advantages. Level mounting facilitates four-hammer playing, whereas the raised back row eases the playing of rapid passages.

Apart from including two additional pairs (hard and medium felt), the beaters for the xylophone are the same as those for the glockenspiel.

Marimba. This is a deep-toned and mellow-sounding xylophone (fully resonated) which should have a range of three and a half octaves or four octaves, descending in either case to one octave below middle C.

The best tone is produced from the marimba with beaters

[1] Recent experiments in bar material include a scientifically formulated silicate of great durability and brilliance.

of medium and hard felt, or medium and soft rubber. Hard beaters rob the instrument of its characteristic tone and do considerable damage to the slender wooden bars.

Vibraphone (Vibraharp). Like the marimba, this instrument is ideally suited to solo playing. Both instruments are also firmly established in modern music, with a definite place in combinations ranging from the chamber ensemble to the symphony orchestra.

There are two types of vibraphone: the tube-resonated type, and the model with electronic amplification, including vibrato, etc. In the first model the vibrato is obtained by the alternate opening and closing of the upper ends of the resonators by means of revolving discs. Both models have alloy bars and foot-controlled damping mechanism. In the orchestra (as in modern jazz) the vibraphone is often used without vibrato.

The 'concert' model with its range of three octaves:

(sounding as written)

suits most purposes. A range of two and a half octaves from middle C upwards is reasonably adequate.

The mallets for the vibraphone are similar to those used on the marimba, with the addition of the slightly heavier worsted or yarn-covered rubber core. Reasonably stiff mallets with longish handles are required for the vibraphone (and marimba) as a good deal of four-hammer work is required on both instruments. Hard beaters are effective on the vibraphone but must be used with discretion.

THE TUBULAR BELLS (ORCHESTRAL CHIMES)

FR. *CLOCHES;* GER. *GLOCKEN (RÖHREN);* IT. *CAMPANE*

A set of eighteen bells mounted chromatically in two rows, off-set, with a range of one and a half octaves: C—F:

(sounding 8ᵛᵃ)

is necessary in the orchestral percussion.

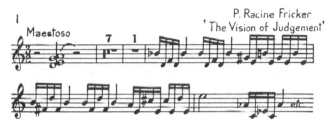

It is customary to hire 'outsize' chimes below middle C or above the high F for works such as the *Symphonie Fantastique* (Berlioz) and certain Russian operas.

One and a half inch diameter bell-metal tubing is recommended, though all sizes from 1 in. to 2 in. have their advantages. (Whilst the characteristic tones of the bell plate, mushroom bell, and amplified wire used by certain large organizations provide admirable bell sounds, such equipment is rarely available to the average orchestral player.)

Foot- and hand-operated damping mechanism is normally fitted to the chromatic set of chimes.

The tube is struck squarely at the top:

Fig. 30

A small rawhide hammer makes an ideal bell mallet. If a leather disc is glued to one end of the mallet head, two distinct tones are possible.

UPKEEP

All the tuned percussion instruments require a fair amount of upkeep. The bars of the glockenspiel and vibraphone tend to tarnish easily. The xylophone notes need attention to keep them in good trim. An occasional wax polishing is a good rejuvenator. An eye should be kept on the suspension cords, rubber buffers, etc. and the resonators occasionally emptied of the dust which accumulates at the bottom of the tube. This tends to sharpen the pitch of the chamber and consequently 'choke' the note. Keep all working parts oiled, particularly the bearings on the vibraphone. Care must be taken when moving and dismantling the xylophone and marimba as the wooden bars are easily chipped.

Wear and tear and adverse climatic conditions subject even the finest and best seasoned wood to slight distortion, with a subsequent change of pitch. Retuning should in all cases be left to the expert. 'Doctoring' the bars to produce the overtones and fundamentals which give the required pitch and brilliance demands the skill of an experienced tuner. There is a good deal more in tuning than shortening the bar to sharpen, and shallowing the underside (arch fashioned) to flatten. Store all instruments in an even temperature.

TECHNICAL APPROACH

All the tuned percussion instruments require a similar technique. Thus the study of one instrument will enable one to give a good performance on the others. Of the five instruments, it is proposed to deal only with the xylophone. If dexterity is achieved on this instrument, the remainder present only small differences in tonal approach.

The grip, etc.

The grip and playing position of the beaters are shown in Fig. 31.

Fig. 31

They are held similarly to the timpani sticks, or the right hand side drum stick. The wrists are turned inwards with the palm facing downwards. The shaft is gripped between the thumb and the first joint of the first finger. The second, third, and fourth fingers are held clear of the handle.

The length of the shaft is governed to a great extent by the immediate requirements, i.e. whether the player is using two, three, or four hammers. For intricate two-hammer playing many professional players prefer shortish handles (approximately 9 in. in length). To enable the beaters to be gripped or manipulated comfortably when the instrument is to be played with four hammers (i.e. two beaters in each hand) the shafts need to be at least 12 in. long. Figs. 32 and 33 show the grip, which is the same in each hand. The way the shafts cross in the palm is arbitrary.

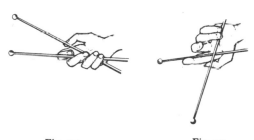

Fig. 32   Fig. 33

The span is extended and reduced by opening and closing the beaters in a scissor-like fashion. The shafts are held together with third and fourth fingers. Pressure with the thumb and first and second fingers alters the distance between the beaters to the required interval (see p.80).

When playing with two beaters the shafts form an angle of ninety degrees. The arms are held straight from elbow to knuckles and slightly clear of the body. The stroke is made with a flicking movement of the wrist. The bars are struck in the centre wherever possible, though to facilitate the playing of rapid passages (for instance chromatic scales) the near ends of the back row notes may be struck.

The normal stance is to stand (or sit) a little to the left of the centre of the xylophone, facing slightly to the right, with the music placed to the right of the centre of the instrument. The music stand must be well clear of the back row of notes, but not so high as to obscure the conductor.

Practice exercises, etc.

The majority of remarks and exercises dealing with the roll, stick manipulation, cross-over beats, etc., on the timpani (see pp.40–46) apply to the xylophone. The sustained note on the xylophone, indicated by the customary three strokes or *tr* (not to be confused with trill), is performed by a series of rapidly reiterating single strokes in the form of a roll. A close roll is required on the xylophone, there being no length to the tone as with the kettledrum.

The basic exercises consist of scales and arpeggios in every possible position, key, and time-signature. Little can be added to the numerous exercises and examples to be found in printed tutors, except to suggest a 'limbering-up' routine by way of a xylophone 'daily dozen'. The suggested Exx. 2–5a should be written out and practised in every key and time signature. As with the side drum and timpani, they should commence slowly and gradually accelerate.[1]

---

[1] The music for all these instruments is usually written in the treble clef, but the bass clef is occasionally used for the marimba and chimes. It would be helpful to most players if music for marimba and chimes was always in the treble clef. It would also be helpful if music for *all* tuned percussion instruments was written as often as possible *in* the stave, so as to reduce the use of leger lines. *8va* or *8va bassa* will indicate the position required on the instrument.

Exx. 6–10 dealing with arpeggios and broken chords should be similarly treated.

The instinctive judging of distance, so absolutely necessary to the xylophonist, is best developed by the practice of octaves and double stops. Exx. 11—15 are typical exercises — they should be extended and played in every key.

Cross-hammering and the double beat

In cross-hammering, the left hammer passes more frequently *over* the right and the right under the left than otherwise. Wherever possible, however, the sticks should move up and down the instrument *without* cross-over beats, particularly when moving from the front to the back row or vice versa. Quite often cross-over beats can be avoided by the use of the double beat. Indeed, many passages that present difficulty if played hand to hand, 'iron out' considerably if the double beat is used. When and where to employ the double beat must be left to the player's judgement. The shape of the passage and the difference in deftness of the right and left hand governs the situation to a great extent. No definite rule can be made.

16ᴬ

Professional players differ in opinion and approach. The hammerings in Ex. 17 from Gershwin's *Porgy and Bess* are those of two eminent orchestral xylophonists (both of whom demonstrated the passage brilliantly to the writer).

17

Four-hammer playing

The technique of three and four-hammer playing is most absorbing. First, the grip and manipulation of the beaters must be thoroughly practised until all the intervals from a semitone to an octave — or more — are spanned comfortably and speedily, with either and both hands. The outward or inward twist of the wrists is determined by the position of the chord and the speed of the changes. As with two-hammer playing, the ends of the back row of notes can be used to help a quick change, and a rapid turn of the wrist can help to reduce or augment an interval without altering the span of the beaters to any extent (as illustrated in Figs. 34 and 35).

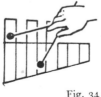

Fig. 34

Fig. 35

Ideally the bars should be struck centrally, but to minimise wrist movement it is often advantageous to strike the ends of the sharps and flats. If a part that is written for three hammers is played with two beaters in each hand, the fourth beater will give greater freedom in positioning the hands. A slight tilt keeps one of the beaters clear of the bars.

Solo playing and sight reading

The xylophone is an attractive solo instrument. There are many excellent xylophone solos which are published with piano or full orchestral accompaniment. Piano, violin, or flute solos, or studies ranging from Bach to present-day composers, make excellent solos and practice material. The practice required to perform solos in public develops the memory, ensures agility, and gives confidence — all of which are important factors in orchestral playing. If the player has even a slight knowledge of the piano, and of musical form, solos are memorized and played more easily. These attributes are invaluable also to the orchestral xylophonist, as they lead to greater understanding of orchestral texture and aid sight reading.

It is important that all the tuned percussion instruments are approached with a picture of the whole keyboard in mind. The reference to the back row as accidentals and the visible lettering of the bars (which is done by many manufacturers) is to be deplored. If aid is sought from the latter in the basic exercises, the desired musical approach to the instruments is obstructed.

Present-day conditions demand that the xylophone is played virtually at sight. In the past, the excellent scoring for the xylophone was mainly sequential and imitative. The majority of these examples were brief and easily memorized. Of late, however, the style of writing for the xylophone has undergone a complete change. The complex and often lengthy passages are frequently exposed, and are extremely difficult to memorize, particularly in the short time usually available. It is essential for the modern xylophonist to develop the technique of sight reading. An example of what might come 'out of the blue' at an orchestral rehearsal may be seen in excerpts from the *Carte Blanche* Ballet Suite by Addison, Constant Lambert's *The Rio Grande* or Tippett's 3rd Symphony.

APPENDIX A

TUTORS AND METHODS

Among others, the following printed tutors are recommended. Quotations from major works appear in the majority of them.

Complete Methods
The Harry A. Bower System. Carl Fischer.
The Gardner Modern Method. Carl Fischer.
Kruger, F. *Pauken und Kleine Trommel-Schule.* E. Parrhysius.
Ludwig, William F. *Complete Drum Instructor.* Ludwig Drum Co.
Studi per Strumenti a Percussione. Aldo & Antonio Buonomo, Edizioni Suvini Zerboni, Milan.

Timpani
Cirone, A.J. *Portraits for Timpani*, Belwin Mills.
Friese-Lepak. *Timpani Method*, Belwin Mills.
Goodman, Saul. *Modern Method for Tympani.* Mills Music Inc.
Hochrainer, Richard. *Etüden für Timpani.* Verlage Doblinger.

Side Drum
Fink, Siegfried. *Percussion Studio*, vols 1-6. Simrock (R. Schauer).
Goldenberg, Morris. *Modern School for Snare Drum.* Chappell.
Keune, Eckehardt. *Schlaginstrumente, Kleine Trommel.* Breitkopf & Härtel.
Lylloff, Bent. *Twenty Four Duets* for Percussionists. Hansen.
Stone, G. *Stick Control for the Snare Drummer.* G.B. Stone Inc. Boston, U.S.A.

Suggested for Beginners
Herfort. *A Tune a Day for Drums.* Chappell.

Xylophone, etc.
Blades, J. *Playing Melodic Percussion.* An Introductory Method. Faber Music Ltd.
Burton, Gary. *Introduction to Jazz Vibes.* Creative Music, Illinois.
Goldenberg, Morris. *Modern School for Xylophone, Marimba, Vibraphone.* Chappell.
Kraus, P. *Modern Mallet Methods.* Henry Adler, New York.

Torrebruno, Leonida. *Metodo per Xilofono e Marimba*. G. Ricordi & Co. Milan.

Veigl, W. *Etüden für Xylophon*. Verlag Doblinger.

Modern-Style Drumming

Abrams, M. *Modern Techniques for the Progressive Drummer*. The Premier Drum Co., London.

Chapin, J. *Advanced Techniques for the Modern Drummer*. Chapin, J., New York.

Grossman, Norman. *The Complete Book of Modern Drumming*. Wise Publications.

Rich-Adler. *Snare Drum Rudiments*. Embassy Music Corporation, New York.

Latin-American Style

Morales, Humberto. *Latin-American Rhythm Instruments and How to Play Them*. Kar-Val Publishing Corporation, New York.

APPENDIX B

WORKS FEATURING PERCUSSION

General

Fanfare for a Joyful Occasion. William Alwyn. O.U.P.

Sonata for two Pianos and Percussion. Bartók. Boosey & Hawkes.

Toccata. Carlos Chávez. Mills Music Inc.

Quotations in Percussion. Arthur Cohn. Mills Music Inc.

Suite for Violin, Piano and Percussion. Alan Hovhaness. Peters.

French Suite (For Percussion Solo). William Kraft. Wolf Mills Music, Los Angeles.

Salmigondis pour timbales, instruments a percussion, et piano. Pierre Petit. Leduc, Paris.

How The Stars Were Made (For Percussion Ensemble). Peter Sculthorpe. Faber Music Ltd.

L'Histoire du Soldat. Stravinsky. J. W. Chester.

Belshazzar's Feast. William Walton. O.U.P.

Ionisation. Edgar Varese. New Music Orchestra Series, San Francisco.

Concertos, etc.

Concerto for Timpani and Orchestra. Harold Farberman. Belwin-Mills, London.

Zyklus. Stockhausen, Universal Edition.

Concerto for Four Percussion Soloists and Orchestra. William Kraft. Belwin Mills, London.

Geigy Festival Concerto. Rolf Liebermann. Universal Edition.

Concerto pour batterie. Darius Milhaud. Universal Edition.

Concerto for Timpani and Orchestra. Werner Thärichen. Ed. Bote & G. Bock, Berlin.

Mytha-Logica for Timpani and Orchestra (or Piano). Karl-Heinz Koper. K H K, Hanover.

Works Featuring Timpani

Symphony No. 1. William Walton. O.U.P.

Symphony in One Movement. Samuel Barber. G. Schirmer Inc.

Nocturne for Tenor and Orchestra. Benjamin Britten. Boosey & Hawkes.

Eight Pieces for Kettledrums. Elliott Carter. Associated Music Publishers Inc.

Sonata for 3 Unaccompanied Kettledrums. Daniel Jones. Peters.

Sonatina for Timpani. (Unaccompanied). Alan Ridout. Boosey & Hawkes.

Sonatina for Two or Three Timpani and Piano. Alexander Tcherepnin. Boosey & Hawkes.

Works Featuring Xylophone, etc.

'Carte Blanche' Ballet Suite. John Addison. O.U.P.

Little Serenade. William Bardwell. Privately printed, Harwell, 1954.

Le Marteau sans Maître. Pierre Boulez. Universal Edition.

Sonata for Xylophone Solo. Thomas B. Pitfield. Peters.

Suite for Xylophone and Orchestra. David Carey. Galaxy Music Corporation, New York.

Concerto for Vibraphone and Marimba. Darius Milhaud. Enoch, Paris.

Tonal Perspective Series for Tuned Percussion (ed. Blades). Boosey & Hawkes.

APPENDIX C

DISCOGRAPHY

Spotlight on Percussion (Demonstrating all percussion including jazz). Vox DL.180.

Bell, Drum and Cymbal (Goodman). Angel 35269.

Percussion in Hi-Fi (Written for six players on all instruments).
   Mercury MG.20166.

Instruments of the Middle Ages and Renaissance. David
   Munrow. E.M.I. (Angel Series) SLS 988.

The Percussive (Examples of tuned percussion and effects).
   Golden Crest CR.3004.

Instruments of the Orchestra IV — Harp and Percussion
   (Demonstrating orchestral percussion instruments). HMV
   Mono 7EG 8675, Stereo GES 5823.

The Instruments of the Orchestra (Sir Adrian Boult). MFP 2092.

Chávez: *Toccata*, and Farberman: *Evolution.* Boston 207.

Siegfried Fink i el seu grup de percussio. Bach-Cage-Caroso-
   Fink, etc. Edigso AZ 70/06.

Blades on Percussion. ABK 13. Discourses Ltd.

Carols for Choirs. The Bach Choir. O.U.P. 150.

RECOMMENDED READING

Percussion Instruments and Their History. Blades, James.
   Faber & Faber.

Early Percussion Instruments. Blades, James and Montagu,
   Jeremy. O.U.P.

Contemporary Percussion. Brindle, Reginald Smith, O.U.P.

The Kettle-Drums. Kirby, Percival. O.U.P. (O/P)

The Art of Tympanist and Drummer. Shivas, Andrew. Dennis
   Dobson.

Handbuch des Schlagzeugs. Peinkoffer and Tannigel, Schott.

World of Percussion. Richards, Emil. Gwyn Publishing Co.
   California.

For current percussion works, see the following journals:

Percussionist. P.A.S. Inc., U.S.A.

Percussion Studio. Benjamin, Hamburg.

Percussive Notes. P.A.S. Inc., U.S.A.

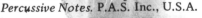